The Quilter's
Edge

Darlene Zimmerman

©2005 Darlene Zimmerman
Published by

krause publications
An Imprint of F+W Publications

700 East State Street • Iola, WI 54990-0001
715-445-2214 • 888-457-2873
www.krausebooks.com

Our toll-free number to place an order or obtain a free catalog is 800-258-0929.

Flip-n-Set™, Easy Scallop™, Easy Rule™, Flex Design Rule™ and Cut & Press I™

Library of Congress Control Number: 2005924837

ISBN-13: 978-0-87349-979-8
ISBN-10: 0-87349-979-4

Edited by Candy Wiza
Designed by Marilyn McGrane and Donna Mummery

Printed in China

Acknowledgments

I would like to thank the following people for their help in making this book possible:

My husband, family and friends, for their continued support.

My editor, Candy Wiza, and all the people at KP Books.

The students in my classes, for their enthusiasm and questions.

Margy Manderfeld, for letting me teach her "Perfect Fit" binding technique.

Lyn Voigt, for the loan of her appliquéd pillow.

EZ Quilting by Wrights, for the manufacture and marketing of my tools.

Robert Kaufman Fabrics, for providing fabrics for the projects.

Bernina, for the loan of a sewing machine.

American and Efird, Inc., for their beautiful threads.

Fairfield Processing Corporation, for supplying the batting for my projects.

June Tailor, Inc., for providing the Cut and Press I.

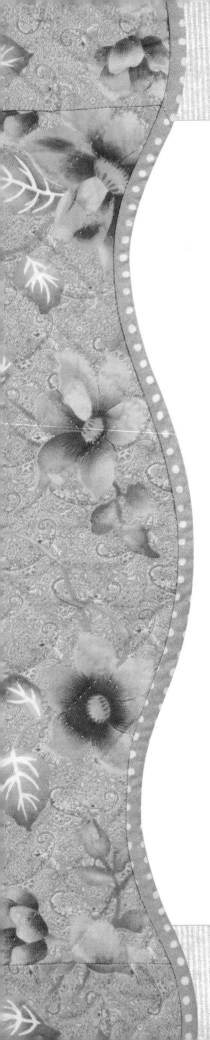

Contents

Introduction

...You have many decisions to make in the process of constructing a quilt. This book is intended to help you with the technical aspects of those decisions ...

Making a quilt is a creative process — even if you are using someone else's pattern. You exercise creativity in your choice of fabrics, the size of the completed quilt, whether or not you choose to use the same setting or borders and how you quilt it and bind it. You have many decisions to make in the process of constructing a quilt. This book is intended to help you with the technical aspects of those decisions: quilt size, setting options, border options and different edge finishes. In this book you will find step-by-step photographs to guide you through the process and to help you achieve the best possible quilt each and every time!

...All the stress is
removed if you
make samples;
any mistakes you
make are learning
experiences and
don't involve
un-sewing,
hair pulling, or
tears!

The different edge finishes and binding techniques taught in this book will widen your repertoire for finishing your quilts. To remove the "fear factor," I suggest you make or purchase some pre-quilted fabric (to simulate a real quilt) and practice the different edge treatments on those samples. Write notes right on the samples for future reference. Practicing on samples will allow you to relax and enjoy learning new techniques, and you can refer back to the samples and notes anytime. All the stress is removed if you make *samples;* any mistakes you make are *learning experiences* and don't involve un-sewing, hair pulling, or tears!

Quilt Sizes

The finished size of the quilt you are making is your decision.

If you are working with a commercial pattern, you may wish to alter the size for various reasons, perhaps to fit a certain bed. Quilt designers are challenged to write patterns to fit beds, as beds (or rather I should say mattresses) come in different sizes. The table on page 9 lists the standardized sizes for beds, comforters and bedspreads, but you need to take into account several factors:

- How thick is your mattress and box spring?

- How much "drop" do you want? ("Drop" is the amount of quilt that hangs down the sides and back of the mattress.)

- Do you want a pillow tuck? (Do you want the quilt to cover the pillows, or will it be tucked under the pillows?)

- Does the bed have a footboard or is it a Hollywood style bed? With a footboard, you may not want much of the quilt to extend beyond the mattress edge. Without a footboard, you will want the same amount of drop as on the sides of the bed.

- The best way to determine the optimal size for your quilt is as follows: Measure the specific bed the quilt is intended for, add the amount of drop you want on the sides and foot of the bed and how much you'll need for the pillow tuck, if you choose to have one.

  - The mattress width + (drop x 2) = width of quilt.

  - The mattress length + pillow tuck + drop at foot of bed = length of quilt.

Table of Common Bed and Quilt Sizes

Standard Mattress Sizes		Comforter	Bedspread
Crib:	27" x 52"		
Twin:	39" x 75"	66" x 89"	80" x 108"
Full:	54" x 75"	82" x 89"	96" x 110"
Queen:	60" x 80"	88" x 94"	102" x 113"
King:	78" x 80"	104" x 94"	118" x 113"
California King:	72" x 84"	100" x 98"	114" x 117"

NOTE: *Heavy* quilting or a puffy batting will take up some of the width and length, slightly shrinking the finished quilt.

Batting companies make their batting in standard sizes and are a helpful guide to a typical quilt size:

Crib: 45" x 60"

Twin: 72" x 90"

Full: 81" x 96"

Queen: 90" x 108"

King: 120" x 120"

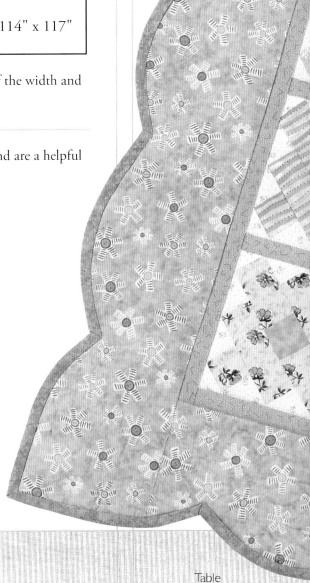

Adjusting the Quilt Size

To make a quilt pattern fit your specifications, you may need to do one of the following:

Make extra blocks.

If you make extra blocks, be aware that the quilt will increase by multiples of the size of the block, plus any sashings. For example: a quilt has 6" finished blocks and 1½" finished sashes. If you make more blocks, the quilt will be increased in size in multiples of 7½". Sometimes adding or subtracting a row or two of blocks to the width and/or length will yield approximately the right size. In some cases you also may need to adjust the width or number of borders to compensate.

If the blocks are set on point (diagonal set), to determine the width and length of a block, multiply the size of the block x 1.414. This will yield the diagonal measurement of the block. (See example.)

> **EXAMPLE**
> 12" block x 1.414 = 16.97
> (or 17").
> If your quilt has five blocks across and six down, it would measure approximately 85"
> (5 x 17") by 102" (6 x 17")
> without borders.

Change the size or number of borders.

Sometimes simply adding a wider or narrower border will allow you to adjust the size of the quilt to fit your specifications. However, be aware that changing the border can affect the visual appeal of your quilt. Adding a 12" border to a quilt to simply make it bigger may not be the best choice — it may look tacked on — not an integral part of the design. Consider instead the addition of several borders. A pieced border or repeating the block in the corners of the borders will bring a color design element from inside the quilt back out to the border.

Change the settings.

Choosing a different method of setting your blocks also can drastically change the size of your quilt. See pages 12 to 47 for a variety of setting options. Setting blocks on point, adding sashing (pieced or plain) or using alternate pieced or plain blocks will make your quilt larger.

Leaving out sashings, alternate blocks or changing a diagonal setting to a straight setting will make your quilt smaller. These are major changes to a quilt, and all the options need to be considered carefully before making a decision. How you set your blocks is the most important decision next to color and design.

Change the size of the blocks.

This again is a rather drastic change — re-sizing the blocks. However, if you prefer the look of a smaller or larger block, it will definitely change the size and the look of your quilt. Making larger blocks will mean you need fewer blocks to yield the same size quilt; with smaller blocks you will need more. If you re-size the blocks, you will probably need to re-size any sashings, alternate blocks and border treatments as well.

Setting Options

Notice the quilts shown on these two pages use the same block, but the position of the color changes as well as the orientation of the blocks.

Blocks can be set any number of different ways. The setting you choose greatly influences the visual appeal of your quilt as well as the size. On the following pages you will find some of the most common setting options available to you, and the pros and cons of each.

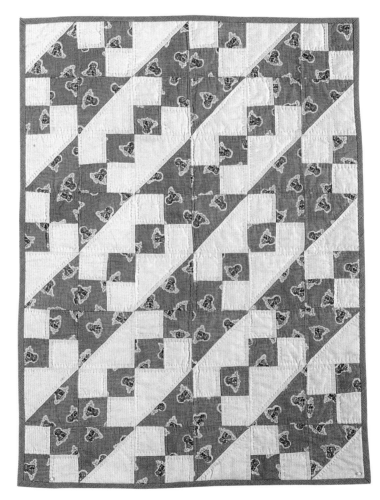

▲Chicken Linen Doll
Granny Quilt Décor

Block-to-Block

This is the most basic of settings, and for certain blocks the most effective. Sometimes the blocks set directly will form secondary designs, or, in order for the blocks to "flow," they need to be set block-to-block. See examples in the quilts on pages 13 to 17.

▲Chicken Linen
Granny Quilt Décor

Block-to-Block

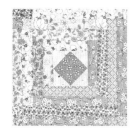

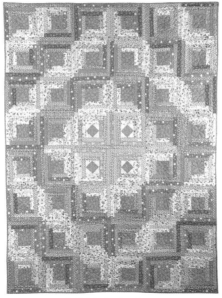

▲Cabin in the Spring
Granny Quilts

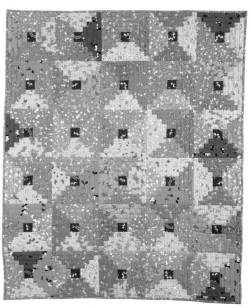

▲Baby Puzzle
Granny Quilts

▲Pineapple Swirl
Granny Quilt Décor

▲Morning Glory
Granny Quilt Décor

▲Feedsack Leaf Quilt
Granny Quilt Décor

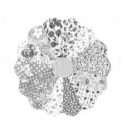

▲Sunny Side Up
Granny Quilts

Appliqué blocks, set block-to-block, will "float" the design on the background fabric, as in Morning Glory, Feedsack Leaf and Sunny Side Up quilts.

Block-to-Block

Some blocks are difficult to sew together block-to-block. It requires matching up seams or points, and, if no secondary design develops when the blocks are set this way, they may benefit from another setting. See the example at right of a block that may NOT look best set block-to-block.

▲Scrappy Delight II
Quick Quilted Miniatures

One way of making a
block-to-block setting
more interesting
is to alternate the
background colors for
the blocks.

▲Dainty Cakestands
Granny Quilt Décor

Asymmetrical Blocks

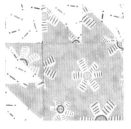

Asymmetrical blocks, such as those shown on pages 18 and 19, often can be interesting when the blocks are turned in multiple directions.

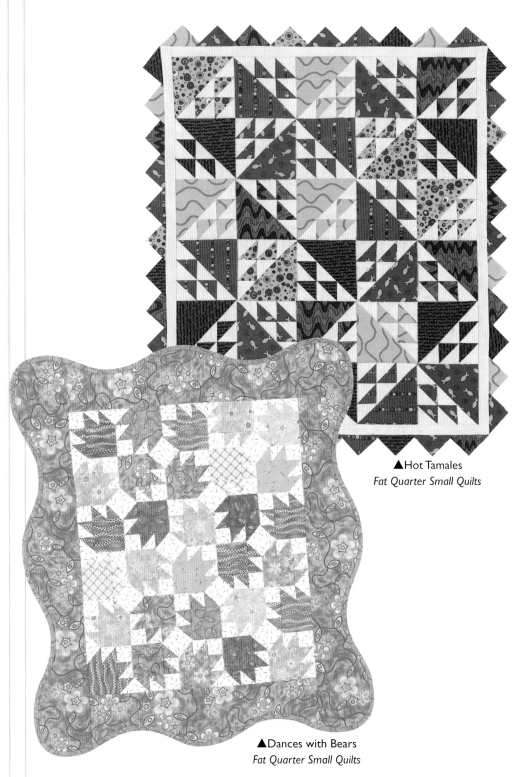

▲Hot Tamales
Fat Quarter Small Quilts

▲Dances with Bears
Fat Quarter Small Quilts

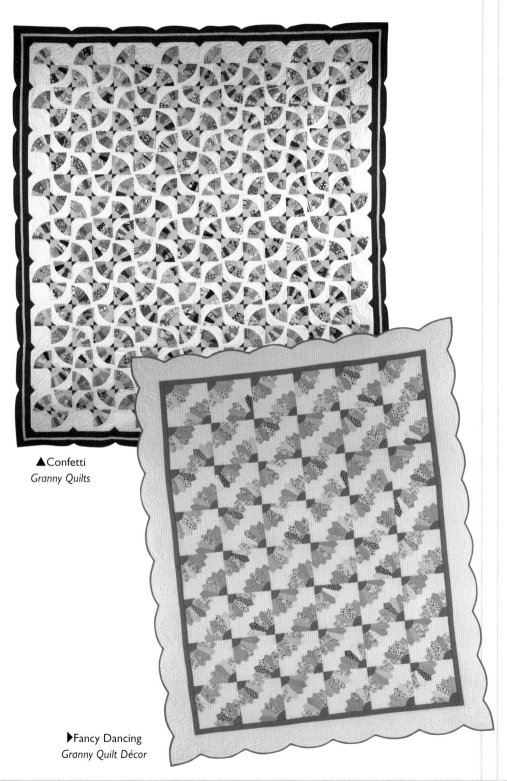

▲Confetti
Granny Quilts

▶Fancy Dancing
Granny Quilt Décor

Blocks with Contrasting Sashing

You will find it easier to set blocks together with some type of sashing between them. It eliminates the need to match up block seams and points. Some blocks look best when "framed" with sashing. The sashing can be a contrasting fabric, as in the following examples:

▲Butterfly Friendship Quilt
Granny Quilts

▲Sweet Lavender
Fat Quarter Small Quilts

▲Feedsack Patches
Granny Quilt Décor

Blocks with Matching Sashing

▲Almost a Flower Garden
Granny Quilt Décor

Or, the sashing can be the same color as the background and the blocks "float."

Sashing with Contrasting Cornerstones

By adding contrasting cornerstones, while the sashing is the same as the block background, you can create a secondary design in the sashing as in Posy Patch.

▲Posy Patch
Fat Quarter Small Quilts

Sashing as a Frame

▲Scrappy Delights
Quick Quilted Miniatures

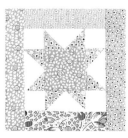

The sashing also can work as a frame, as in Scrappy Delights. Note how the sashings are added around each block like borders on a quilt. This is a great option for a set of blocks that may not all be the same size. Sew the sashings around each block, then trim each block to the same size.

Pieced Block in the Sashing

If you are setting together nine-patch blocks, you also can piece a block into the sashing, as in Aunt Maggie's Quilt, thereby making the blocks float, as well as making the quilt look more interesting.

▲ Aunt Maggie's Quilt
Granny Quilts

Pieced Sashings

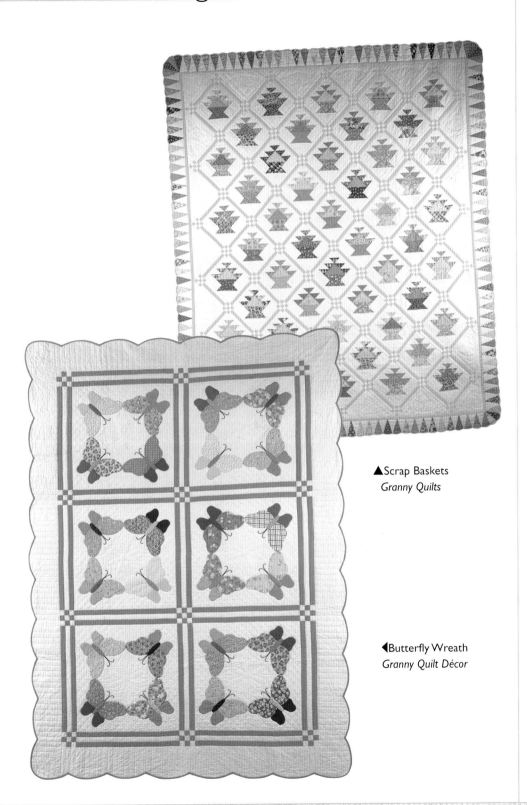

▲Scrap Baskets
Granny Quilts

◀Butterfly Wreath
Granny Quilt Décor

Still another option is a pieced sashing. Note Scrap Baskets and Butterfly Wreath use the same pieced sashing, but the colors are reversed, giving it a different look entirely. Check out pages 26 and 27 for additional quilts with pieced sashings.

Pieced Sashings

▲Picnic Basket Cherries
Granny Quilt Décor

▶Lavender Ladies
Granny Quilts

◀Whimsy
Granny Quilts

Pieced Sashings

Plain Alternate Blocks

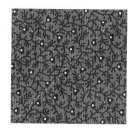

To reduce the number of pieced or appliquéd blocks, set them with alternate blocks. An alternate block can be as simple as a square of fabric in a print or solid color that is the same size as your pieced or appliquéd block.

▲Cinnamon Pink
Fat Quarter Small Quilts

▲Swingin' Babes
Granny Quilt Décor

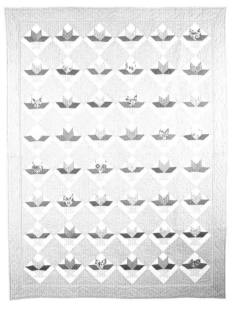

▲Primrose Baskets
Granny Quilts

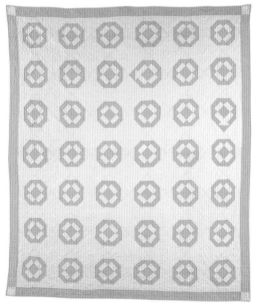

▲Butter and Eggs
Granny Quilt Décor

Pieced Alternate Blocks

For a more interesting effect, an alternate block can be pieced, creating a secondary design. By using a nine-patch as an alternate block, you can create the illusion of a chain, as in Pansies in Bloom.

▲Pansies in Bloom
Fat Quarter Small Quilts

◀Peppermint Twist
Fat Quarter Small Quilts

Nine-Patch Alternate Blocks

Taking the nine-patch alternate block a step further, piece an expanded version of a nine-patch or use sashing and alternate blocks together for an even better chain effect. They will give the illusion the quilt blocks are set in a diagonal setting. In Gingham Flowers the sashing is the same fabric as the background of the blocks, making the blocks "float."

◀Peek-a-Boo Baskets
Granny Quilts

▶Gingham Flowers
Fat Quarter Small Quilts

Double Nine-Patch Alternate Blocks

Taking the nine-patch block a step further, you can piece a *double* nine-patch as shown in Parasol Ladies at left.

TIP: To figure the size strip/squares to cut for any nine-patch, divide the finished block size by 3. Add ½" for seam allowances and cut that size strip/squares.

EXAMPLE
6" finished block divided by 3 = 2" + ½" = 2½" strip/square.

Hourglass Alternate Blocks

An hourglass block set between pieced blocks can give the illusion of stars pieced in the background.

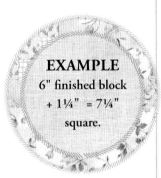

EXAMPLE
6" finished block
+ 1¼" = 7¼"
square.

TIP: To figure what size triangles to cut for the hourglass block, take the finished size of the block and add 1¼". Cut a square that size and cut twice on the diagonal. See example.

▲Buttercup
Fat Quarter Small Quilts

Alternate Connector Blocks

◀Star Flowers
Fat Quarter Small Quilts

▲Lemon Twist
Granny Quilts

A plain square or rectangle with corners added (sometimes called a "connector block") is another great way to set off your pieced blocks and/or create a secondary design.

◀A Tisket A Tasket
Fat Quarter Small Quilts

Connector Block Formula

Connector blocks are easy to make. To add corners to a square or rectangle, mark the diagonal on the wrong side of the smaller squares. Place on the corner of the larger squares or rectangles and sew on the diagonal line. Trim the seam to ¼" and press toward the corner.

The formula for figuring the size of connector corners is as follows: Take the *finished* size of the block, divide by 2, then add ½" for seam allowances.

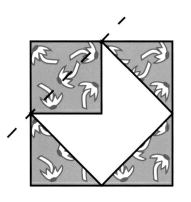 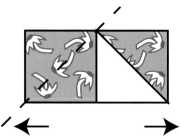

EXAMPLE
6" finished block divided by 2 = 3" + ½" = 3½" squares for the corners of the blocks.

TIP: If possible, choose a square size different from the units in your pieced blocks to avoid having to match up seams or points on the main blocks (see Star Flowers on page 33 for an example).

Strippy Setting

One setting, not commonly used any longer, is called a "strippy setting" — the blocks are set in long vertical rows, separated by sashing. While easy to piece, it is important all the strips finish to the same length!

There are many other alternate blocks or different ways to sash blocks — the possibilities are endless! Explore some of these possibilities with your next quilt project.

◀Vintage Doll Quilt
Fat Quarter Small Quilts

▶Grandma's Strippy Quilt
Granny Quilts

Diagonal Settings

You can use any of
the setting options
given on pages 36
through 41 when
setting blocks on
point. The advantages
to setting blocks on
point are ...

... The blocks often
look more interesting
on point. See
example at right.

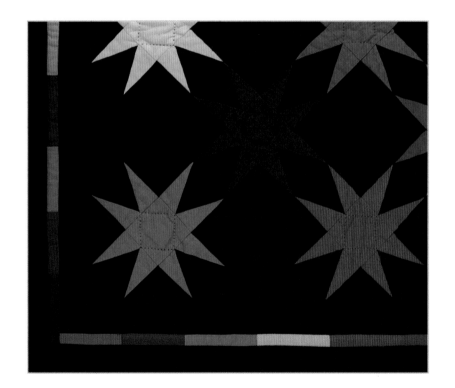

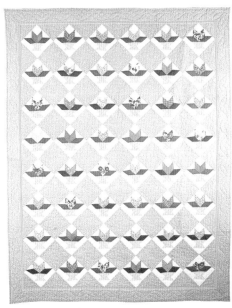

▲Primrose Basket
Granny Quilts

▲Grandmother's Fan
Granny Quilts

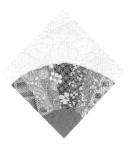

... Some blocks, such
as baskets or fans,
look better when the
block is on point.

◀Bride's Bouquet
Granny Quilts

Diagonal Settings

Diagonal Settings

... It does not take as many blocks to make a quilt. Some examples of block-to-block settings on the diagonal are found at right.

Block-to-Block on Point

▲Under the Sea
Fat Quarter Small Quilts

▲Batik Baskets
Fat Quarter Small Quilts

Diagonal Settings

... It will require even fewer pieced or appliquéd blocks if you set them with alternate plain blocks. Spinning Stars I and Butter and Eggs are examples of quilts set on point with alternate plain blocks.

▲Spinning Stars I
Fat Quarter Small Quilts

▲Butter and Eggs
Granny Quilt Décor

Diagonal Settings

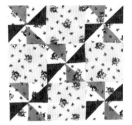

... Using different
colors or fabrics
for the alternate
blocks and setting
triangles can produce
interesting results.

Block-to-Block with Alternate Blocks on Point

▲Sunshine and Lavender
Fat Quarter Small Quilts

▲Baskets and Posies
Fat Quarter Small Quilts

...An alternate block
can be any pieced or
appliquéd block, but
it should complement
the first block, not
compete with it for
attention.

▶Peppermint Twist
Fat Quarter Small Quilts

Diagonal Settings

Diagonal Settings

... Blocks set on point also can benefit from plain or pieced sashings, as shown on the following quilts.

Diagonal Settings with Sashing

▲ Bride's Bouquet
Granny Quilts

▲Scrap Baskets
Granny Quilts

Diagonal Settings

...Blocks on point also can be set in long vertical rows — a strippy setting.

Blocks on Point with Strippy Setting

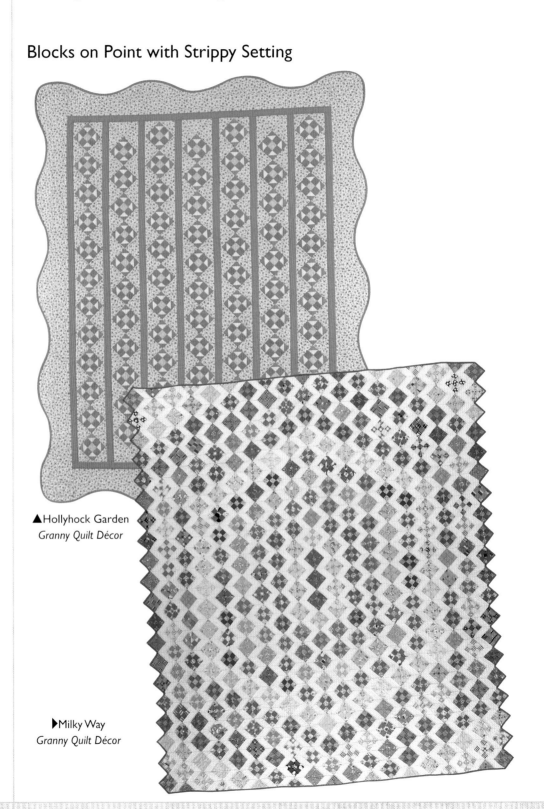

▲Hollyhock Garden
Granny Quilt Décor

▶Milky Way
Granny Quilt Décor

▲Grandma's Strippy Quilt
Granny Quilts

Formulas

The examples
on the following
pages promise to
be a quilt-making
formula for
success!

▲Large Wedding Ring
Quick Quilted Miniatures

▲Under the Sea
Fat Quarter Small Quilts

Setting Triangles

To determine what size to cut quarter-square setting triangles (triangles along the edge of a quilt set on point) take the finished size of the block, multiply by 1.414. Take that answer and add 1.25. Take that answer, round it up to the nearest ½" and cut a square that size. Cut the square twice on the diagonal.

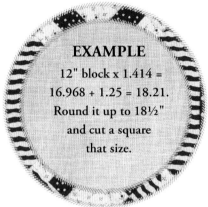

EXAMPLE

12" block x 1.414 =
16.968 + 1.25 = 18.21.
Round it up to 18½"
and cut a square
that size.

OR — if you prefer NOT to do the required math, you can use a tool called Flip-n-Set that will cut triangles from a strip of fabric, no math involved!

1 Find the finished size of the blocks on the tool. Read across to find the strip size to cut.

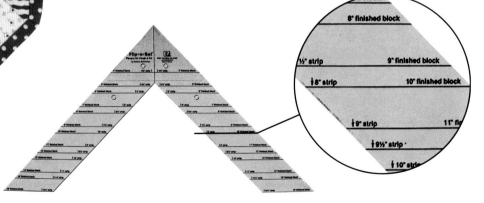

2 Lay the tool on the opened strip (cut singly). Align the tool at the correct strip size at the bottom of the fabric strip and the tip of the tool at the top of the fabric strip. Cut along one side and down the other.

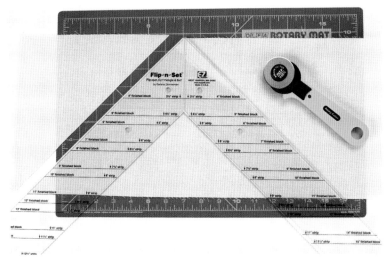

3 Reverse the tool. Align the tool's correct strip size to the top of the fabric strip, the angled cut edge, and the point at the bottom of the fabric strip. Cut again on the right side. Continue in this manner across the fabric strip.

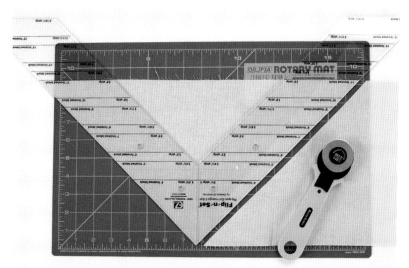

4 Cutting corner triangles is covered in the next section.

Diagonal Setting with Sashes

If you have blocks in a diagonal setting with sashes, you also will need to add the *finished* width of *one* sashing to the block size to determine the size of triangles.

You also can use Flip-n-Set to cut these larger triangles.

EXAMPLE

12" block + 2" finished sashing = 14" block. Use that size to determine the correct strip size to cut for Flip-n-Set.

Or, if NOT using Flip-n-Set, take the size of the block, add the finished size of one sashing, and multiply by 1.414. Take that answer and add 1.25. Round up that answer to the nearest ½". Cut a square that size; cut it twice on the diagonal.

EXAMPLE

12" block + 2" sashing = 14" block x 1.414 = 19.796 + 1.25 = 21.04. Round up to 21½", cut a square that size and cut twice on the diagonal.

You also can use the table below to give you the sizes of squares to cut if you are NOT using Flip-n-Set.

Setting Triangles Table

Block Size	Square Size	Block Size	Square Size
4"	7"	12"	18½"
5"	8½"	13"	20"
6"	10"	14"	21½"
7"	11½"	15"	22½"
8"	13"	16"	24"
9"	14"	17"	25½"
10"	15½"	18"	27"
11"	17"		

Corner Triangles

The corners of a quilt set on the diagonal are different from the setting triangles. They are called *half-square triangles* and are cut differently. I recommend cutting two squares the size of your finished block. Cut once on the diagonal to make four corner triangles.

All the triangles are cut a bit oversized so you can trim the edge straight, leaving a ¼" seam allowance (or more if you want your blocks to float) along the edge.

TIP: Use Flip-n-Set to help square up the corners of your quilt. It is nearly 18" long on two adjacent sides.

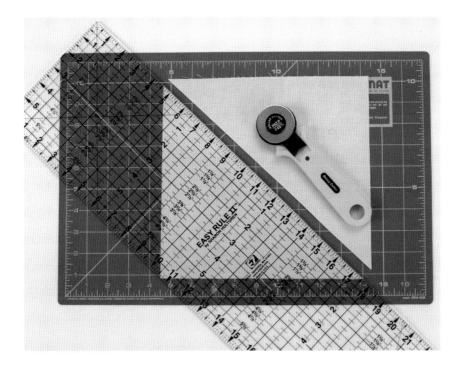

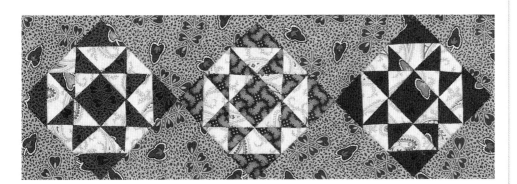

An example of corner triangles.

Square Up a Quilt

Remember to leave at least ¼" from the corners of the blocks for seam allowance. You may choose to leave more to "float" your blocks.

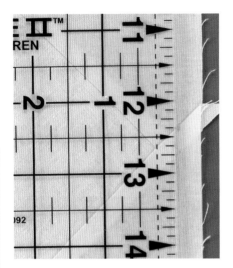

If you have set your blocks on point, and cut the setting triangles slightly larger than needed, you will need to square up your quilt before adding borders or binding. You can use either Flip-n-Set or a large square and a chalk marker (whatever color will show up on your quilt).

Lay as much of the quilt as possible flat on a table. Starting in one corner, position your large square or Flip-n-Set over the corner; make sure you have at least a ¼" seam allowance from the corners of the blocks. Mark the outside edge with the chalk marker. (Do not cut at this point, you may need to adjust slightly.) Repeat at all four corners of the quilt. With your ruler and chalk, mark the edges between the corners, again leaving at least a ¼" seam allowance from the corners of the blocks. Adjust the chalk lines as needed. When satisfied the quilt is marked as square as possible, use a rotary cutter and ruler to trim off the excess quilt edge.

Calculate Your Quilt Size

To figure the *finished* size of your quilt, add the following measurements:

Width: The *finished* size of your blocks times the number of blocks across PLUS the finished size of the sashing times the number of sashes across (usually one less than the number of blocks) PLUS the finished border widths times 2.

EXAMPLE
10" block **x** 5 blocks
across = **50"**.
2" sashing **x** 4 = **8"**.
4" borders **x** 2 = **8"**.
50"(blocks) + **8"**(sashings)
+ **8"**(borders) = **66"**.
The finished width of
the quilt is 66".

Counting the blocks, sashes and border lengthwise of the quilt, figure the length in the same manner as you calculated the width.

Length: 10" block **x** 6 blocks down = **60"**. 2" sashing **x** 5 = **10"**. 4" borders **x** 2 = **8"**. **60"**(blocks) + **10"**(sashings) + **8"**(borders) = **78"**. The finished length of the quilt is 78".

To figure the finished size of a quilt with the blocks set on point, take the block size times 1.414 to find the width of the block across the diagonal. Follow the steps outlined above using that diagonal measurement.

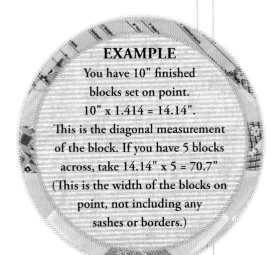

EXAMPLE
You have 10" finished
blocks set on point.
10" x 1.414 = 14.14".
This is the diagonal measurement
of the block. If you have 5 blocks
across, take 14.14" x 5 = 70.7"
(This is the width of the blocks on
point, not including any
sashes or borders.)

Borders

Consider the border to be the "frame" around your quilt. Just as a picture or artwork deserves a frame to enhance it, so does your quilt. The border can be simple strips of fabric of an appropriate width, or you can add multiple borders or pieced borders for a more interesting look.

Borders can be sewn using either of the following methods: Sew top and bottom borders first, then side borders **OR** sides first, then the top and bottom. Either way is acceptable.

Lengthwise or Widthwise Borders?

Borders can be cut from the width or the length of the fabric. Cutting border strips lengthwise (parallel to the selvage) will eliminate the need to piece the borders. It is a good choice for a large print or floral, but it usually requires more fabric. Borders cut across the width, from selvage to selvage, may need to be pieced to fit the quilt. Usually the piecing is done at a 45-degree angle to hide the seam, but sometimes it's less visible with a straight seam. Choose what is right for your fabrics!

To join two borders with a diagonal seam, place them right sides together at right angles (an "L" shape) to each other. Mark a line from the corner of one border to the corner of the other border strip. Sew on that line; trim the seam to ¼" and press the seam open.

Borders cut lengthwise will stretch less than those cut across the width. Consider this aspect when deciding how to cut your borders. I find a quilt set on point has considerable stretch. Borders cut widthwise also have a bit of stretch. Sewing borders cut widthwise to a quilt set on point will prevent the pieced center from sagging outward. Some quilters prefer using lengthwise borders, as they feel it stabilizes their quilt.

To figure the yardage needed (or number of strips to cut) for borders cut across the *width*, take the total measurement of all the borders and divide by 40. Round to the nearest whole number. This will tell you how many strips to cut. To figure yardage, multiply the number of strips you have to cut by the width of the borders. See example 1.

To figure yardage for borders cut *lengthwise*, use the length of the longest border plus a few inches for insurance. If you'd like to make use of the extra fabric in the blocks or sashing, cut the borders first (adding a few inches for "insurance" or including border widths) then you can use the remainder of the fabric for blocks or sashes in the quilt. See example 2. Sew the longest borders to the quilt first.

EXAMPLE 1
The quilt measures 56" x 70" (before borders are added) and the borders are cut at 4½".
56" + 70" = 126" x 2 = 252"
+ 18" (4 border widths) = 270".
(270" is the total perimeter of the quilt.)
270" divided by 40" = 6.75 (round up to 7 strips).
Cut (7) 4½" x 42" strips for the borders.
7 x 4½" = 31.5"
(Round up to 1 yd.)

EXAMPLE 2
The quilt measures 56" x 70" and you are adding borders cut at 4½". If you add the side borders (length) first, then you need 70" total — or 2 yd. (You will have 2" extra, but it's a wise idea to have slightly more fabric than the total length for "insurance.")

Simple Borders

Frequently, simple borders are added with butted seams at the corners. To assure proper fit of borders, measure your quilt through the middle (the edge may have stretched) in several places. Take an average of that measurement if necessary. Cut two borders to this length. Mark the centers of the borders and the quilt top. Pin, working from the centers out. Sew and press toward the borders. Repeat this procedure on the remaining two sides of the quilt, including the measurements of the borders just added.

TIP: You can save time by using the border strips to measure across the quilt. Simply lay the borders on the quilt top as you would a measuring tape and crease to indicate the proper length. Trim the border lengths slightly beyond the crease, allowing a little bit extra for "insurance."

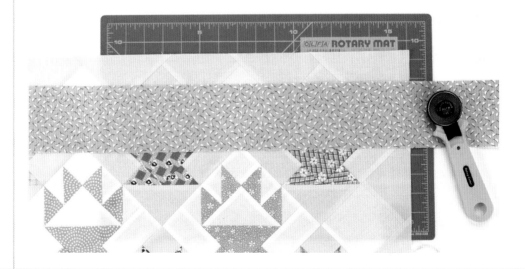

Borders with a Flange

Occasionally one needs just a tiny bit of contrasting color in the border. This is the perfect time to use a flange. To make a very narrow flange, cut straight-of-grain strips ¾" wide, fold in half lengthwise, right-side out, and press.

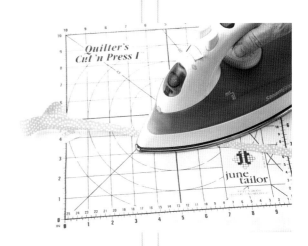

Match the raw edges of the flange to the raw edge of the quilt. Machine baste in place with a scant ¼" seam, simply overlapping at the corners.

Sew the borders to the quilt with an exact ¼" seam. Press. (Note: It is critical to sew this seam as accurately as possible to ensure an even amount of flange showing on the finished project.)

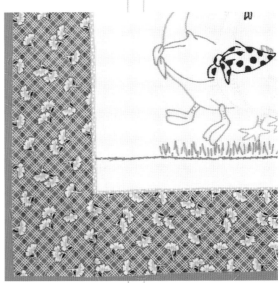

Borders with a Border Print

Lovely border prints (those intended for borders, or a lovely striped fabric) can enhance the quilt tremendously, but need to look good at the corners. How to do this?

Cut (and piece if necessary) the border strips at least 6" longer than needed (see formula on page 57). Lay the border strips on adjacent edges of the quilt and play with the motif corner arrangement until you find the look you want. The border length will then have to be adjusted in the center of the border — you will have to cut the border in half and sew it back together in the center of each border.

Or, you can choose a motif from the border to center in the middle of your quilt, and have the corners work out how they may. Be sure to have *opposite borders* arranged the same way.

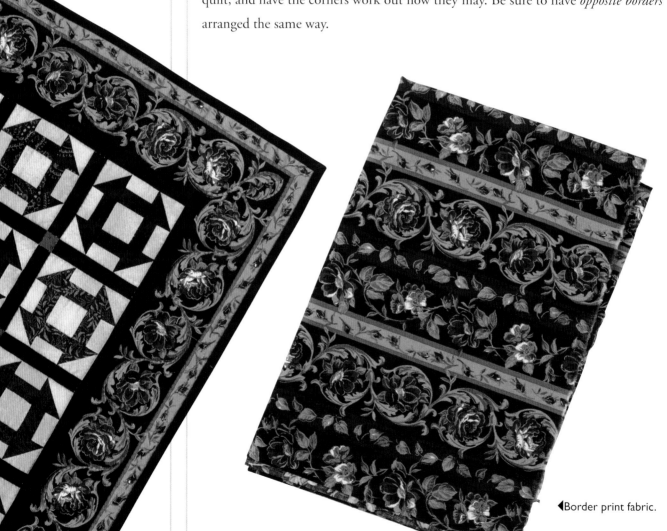

◀Border print fabric.

Mitered Corners on Borders

A mitered border can add an elegant corner finish to your quilt. It is a good choice when you have multiple borders, border fabric that makes the seam highly visible, or if you are matching a design in a border print.

When cutting border lengths, you need to add the length of the quilt plus two border *widths* plus 2" to 4" for extra insurance. On the border strip, mark the center and the quilt width evenly from the center. Match to the quilt top and pin in place, having excess fabric equally at both ends. Stitch only to within ¼" from the corners and backstitch. Repeat this procedure for all sides of the quilt.

EXAMPLE
Quilt measures 56",
borders measure 4½".
56" + 4½" + 4½"
+ 4" = 69"

Tip: When adding multiple borders to a quilt, it might be timesaving to sew the various borders together before sewing them onto the quilt, then miter the corners.

After the borders are stitched on, fold the quilt with right sides together, aligning the raw edges of the borders. With a ruler, mark a 45-degree line from the point where the stitching stopped on the border to the raw edge of the border. Pin and sew on this line, backstitching at both ends. Before trimming the seam allowance, check on the right side to ensure the corner is sewn correctly.

1. Mark the corner.

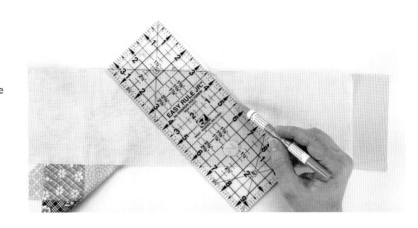

2. Pin corners together.

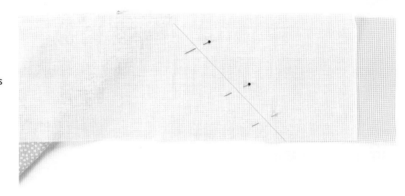

3. Sew the seam.

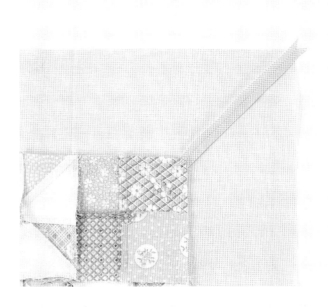

Backside of
sewn seam.

Finished
border seam.

Pieced Borders

Pieced borders can take your quilt from ordinary to extraordinary! Consider this option when making decisions about borders. A pieced border can take elements from the blocks. A Dresden Plate quilt can incorporate an ice cream cone border, or a quilt with lots of triangles can be framed with a sawtooth border.

▲Sunny Side Up
Granny Quilts

▲Hugs and Kisses
Granny Quilts

A pieced border also can echo the colors or prints of the blocks, bringing some color to the outside of the quilt.

▶Feedsack Patches
Granny Quilt

◀Peek-a-Boo Baskets
Granny Quilts

Avoiding Pieced Borders?

Do you avoid pieced borders because you are afraid they won't fit properly? Yes, it can happen to anyone. If there is a slight variation in the cutting or sewing, it can be multiplied many times over in the border. There is a way to make those borders fit without tears! Simply add an inside border (same as the background so it floats, or contrasting to set off the pieced border) slightly *larger* than it needs to be mathematically. Then, piece your borders and measure them up to the quilt (see Simple Borders on page 58). The quilt should now be slightly bigger than the borders. Trim the quilt *evenly* for the pieced borders to fit the quilt. Do this on all four sides before adding the borders. You will need to add another unit or cornerstone to finish out the corner on the last two borders. Look closely at Almost a Flower Garden and you will see the pieced border was added with this method.

▲Almost a Flower Garden
Granny Quilt Décor

Binding

Binding Secrets

There is a secret to binding a quilt ... and having the edge lie flat when finished. The secret is — basting! Hand baste the edge of the quilt a scant ¼" from the edge of the quilt before sewing on the binding. It can be basted with a walking foot and a long stitch on your machine, but I prefer hand basting. Basting the edge before binding prevents the layers from shifting, as well as making sure the edge does not ripple. It's preferable to hand baste the edge while the quilt is lying on a flat surface, such as a large table. You'll be able to see at a glance if the edge is lying flat.

Also, I never trim my quilt until AFTER the binding is sewn on. If the edge doesn't appear to be straight, mark a straight line as a positioning guide for the binding, or simply pull the binding straight as you are sewing it on. Once the binding is sewn on, go back and trim the backing and batting with a scissors. Trim a couple of inches first, then check to see if you have allowed adequate batting and backing to "fill up" the binding. You easily can adjust the amount you trim off with a scissors.

If you use cotton or wool batting (polyester batting can melt) steam-press the edge of the quilt after the binding is finished. The edge will lie flat and straight.

Carefully consider the fabric choice for the binding. Usually a fabric in the body of the quilt or the border is used, but sometimes you can utilize a stripe, plaid or checked fabric on the bias for a striking effect. Some quilts also benefit from a solid-colored binding (which makes more of a statement than a print) or a *contrasting* binding. I generally use a contrasting binding on a scalloped or shaped edge.

Binding Choices

Binding can be single- or double-fold, bias or straight-of-grain. It can match or contrast with the border. It can be narrow — ¼" finished, or wide, up to 1" or more. The choices are yours!

Double bias binding is generally recommended for use on bed quilts, as it wears better than either a single bias binding or a straight-of-grain binding.

If you are running short of binding fabric, or only binding a wall hanging, a single straight-of-grain binding is sufficient.

Single Binding

Cut the fabric strips 1¼" wide for a single-fold bias or straight-of-grain binding. Sew a ¼" seam for a ¼" finished edge.

If you'd like a wider single binding, take the finished width of the binding times 4 plus ¼".

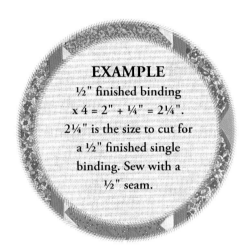

EXAMPLE
½" finished binding x 4 = 2" + ¼" = 2¼". 2¼" is the size to cut for a ½" finished single binding. Sew with a ½" seam.

Double Binding

Cut the binding strips 2¼" wide and sew a ¼" seam for a finished double-fold bias or double-fold straight-of-grain ¼" finished binding.

Double Binding

Finished Width	Cut Size
¼"	2¼"
⅜"	2½"
½"	3½"
⅝"	4¼"
¾"	4¾"
1"	6½"

Note: A puffy or flannel quilt may need a wider binding.

Cutting Bindings

Cutting Straight-of-Grain Bindings (Single- or Double-Fold)

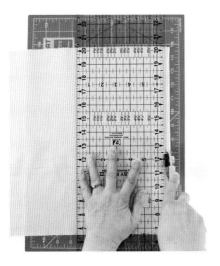

1 With the fabric folded, as it comes off the bolt, straighten the edge. Trim off selvages, as they may pucker in the quilt.

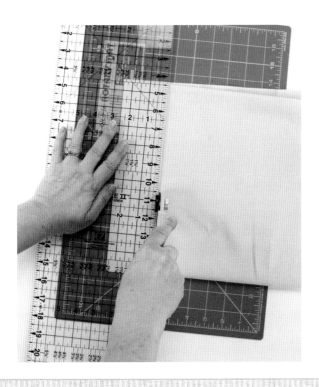

2 Cut strips the width needed for the binding. For number of strips to cut, see formulas and table, page 74, for calculating yardage for cutting binding.

Cutting Bias-Binding Strips (Single- or Double-fold)

1 Trim both raw edges of the fabric piece. Trim off the selvages.

2 Open up the fabric so you are cutting only one layer. Cut off one corner at a 45-degree angle. (You have this marking on your ruler.) Align the 45-degree line with the short edge of your fabric and trim off one corner. (The corner is discarded, or saved for another project.)

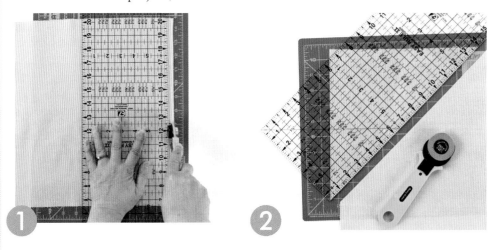

3 Cut bias strips to the desired width. To facilitate cutting, fold over the 45-degree edge to shorten the cut.

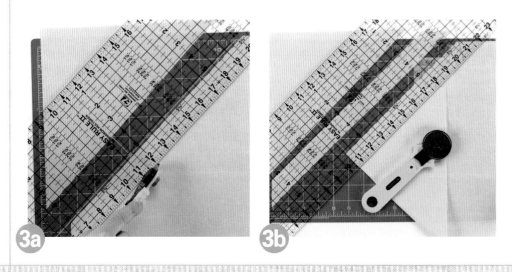

Binding Formulas

Use the example here and the binding chart below and you have a formula for binding success!

EXAMPLE
52"(width)
+ 68"(length)
= 120" x 2 = 240"
+ 12" = 252"
of binding.

To determine how much binding to make, add the measurement of the width of the quilt plus the length of the quilt and multiply by 2. Add 12" extra for turning corners.

Determine how much binding to make for a scalloped or wavy edge by using the same procedure as for a quilt with straight edges; just allow one to two extra yards of binding. Or, to figure the measurement more accurately, "measure" with a length of string along the top and one side of the quilt, following the curves, then measure the string with a ruler and multiply by 2. Add 12" for corners/ending.

To figure the amount of fabric for sraight-of-grain binding, divide the total length (see above) by 40". Round up to the nearest whole number. This is the number of strips you need to cut. (Example: 252 ÷ 40 = 6.3 or 7.)

To figure yardage, multiply the number of strips by the binding width. Round up to the nearest ¼ yd. or ⅛ yd. (Example: 7 strips x 2½" [binding width] = 17.5" = ½ yd. or ⅝ yd.)

To figure the amount of yardage needed for bias binding, see the Binding Table.

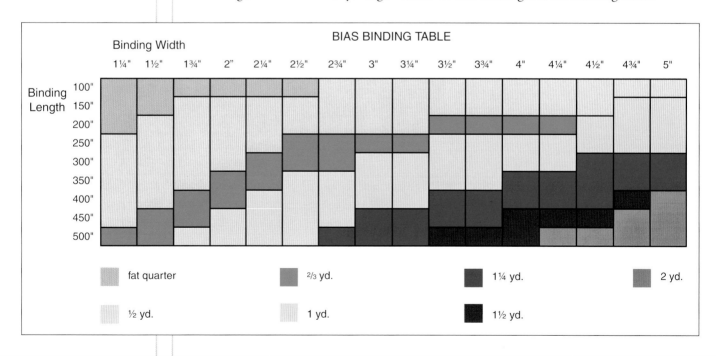

BIAS BINDING TABLE

Binding Width: 1¼" 1½" 1¾" 2" 2¼" 2½" 2¾" 3" 3¼" 3½" 3¾" 4" 4¼" 4½" 4¾" 5"

Binding Length: 100" 150" 200" 250" 300" 350" 400" 450" 500"

Legend:
- fat quarter
- ½ yd.
- ⅔ yd.
- 1 yd.
- 1¼ yd.
- 1½ yd.
- 2 yd.

Binding Preparation

1 Whether single- or double-fold, bias or straight-of-grain, binding ends are joined with diagonal seams pressed open. This will reduce the "bump" in the binding when it is sewn to the quilt.

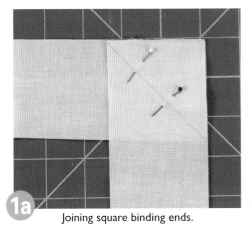

1a Joining square binding ends.

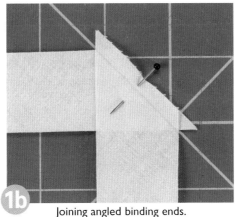

1b Joining angled binding ends.

NOTE: When joining angled ends, offset the ends by ¼". Sew from the "V" where the ends meet to the opposite "V".

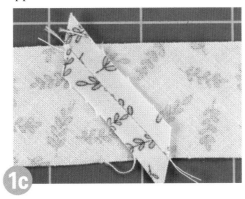

1c

Close-up of diagonal seam pressed open.

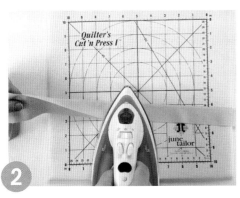

2 To make a double binding, either bias or straight-of-grain, fold the binding in half lengthwise with *wrong* sides together and press.

NOTE: Do not stretch the binding while ironing.

TIP: It might be a wise idea to make the binding when the quilt top is completed, even before it's quilted. Sometime there's a time lag (anything from a few days to a few years!) between finishing a quilt top and getting it quilted, and in the meantime the binding fabric could get lost or used in another project. Cut and prepare the binding when the quilt top is completed, then store together, so when the quilting is finished you are ready to bind.

TIP: The binding can be wrapped around a wide ruler or cardboard, then slipped off for flat storage.

Sewing Bindings

Sewing a Single Straight-of-Grain Binding to a Straight Edge Quilt

Single straight-of-grain binding is sufficient for a small wall hanging or table runner. The small scale of the quilt does not call for a bulky binding, and the edge won't have heavy use, as in a bed quilt.

Single bias binding is a must when binding a scalloped, curved or shaped edge. Bias binding is necessary for curved edges, and single binding is a good choice for scalloped edges, as it eliminates some of the bulk in the "V" of the scallop. Yes, it will wear out more quickly than a double bias binding, but it will be much easier to sew on a scalloped edge. Generally quilters give away most of their quilts, so if the binding wears out it's not their problem!

To stitch a single or double straight-of-grain binding to a straight edge of a quilt, follow these steps:

1 Quilt as desired. Hand baste a scant ¼" from the edge of the quilt to hold the layers together and keep them from shifting. See Binding Secrets page 69.

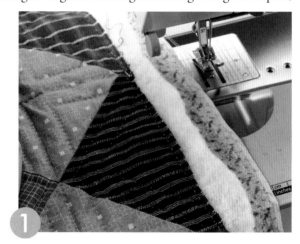

2 Match the raw edge of the binding to the raw edge of the quilt top. Start in the middle of one side, remembering to leave an 8" tail. Stitch the binding with a ¼" quilting foot, sewing a ¼" seam (or wider if the strips are wider).

3 Miter the corners (see Mitering Corners page 79).

4 End the binding with a "Perfect Fit" binding technique (see page 80).

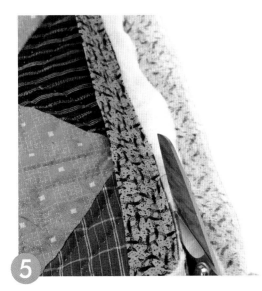

5 Trim the excess batting and backing.

6 On the top side of the quilt, press the binding away from the edge of the quilt to make the binding easier to fold.

7 Fold the binding under ¼" and stitch the binding down by hand with single thread matching the binding. Stitch down with a blind hemstitch, making sure the stitches don't show on the front of the quilt.

TIPS:

• Use appliqué sharp needles for hand stitching the binding — they are nice thin needles designed for this type of stitching.

• When stitching the binding down by hand, keep the body of the quilt away from you. Hold only the binding edge and you'll find it easier to stitch.

• Use binding clips to hold the binding edge down for sewing instead of pins and you won't stick yourself!

A bias binding has many threads going over the edge of the quilt. A straight-of-grain binding will fold on the fabric grain, and wear more quickly.

Sewing a Double Straight-of-Grain Binding to a Straight Edge Quilt

Prepare the quilt edge by basting a scant ¼" from the edge of the quilt. Prepare the double straight-of-grain binding by piecing together with diagonal seams pressed open, then pressing in half lengthwise with wrong sides together. (See Binding Preparation on page 75.)

A double straight-of-grain binding can be used for any straight quilt edge. A *bias* double binding is recommended for bed quilts because of its durability. To apply a double straight-of-grain binding, align the raw edges of the binding to the raw edge of the quilt. Start in the middle of one side and leave an 8" tail. Stitch until you reach the corner; miter the corners. (See Mitering Corners on page 79.)

To end the binding, see "Perfect Fit" binding technique (page 80).

After the binding has been sewn on, trim off excess batting and backing and turn the binding to the wrong side. Stitch down by hand with thread matching the binding. The binding should cover the line of stitching on the backside of the quilt. The hand stitches should not come through to the front of the quilt. See tips for stitching the binding down by hand (page 77).

Mitered Corners on Binding

1 To miter, stitch to within a seam's allowance from the corner (this could be ¼" or wider, depending upon the width you have chosen) stop and backstitch.

2 Remove the quilt from under the presser foot and trim threads. Turn the quilt 90 degrees to begin stitching the next edge of the quilt.

A quilt with square corners will need mitered binding corners.

3 Fold the binding on the diagonal, pull it straight up, then fold back down, with the fold on the previous edge of the quilt.

4 This automatically builds in enough extra binding to turn the corner. When finished, there will be a nice mitered fold at the corner.

"Perfect Fit" Binding

To join the binding ends without a lump, and without being able to tell where you have started, follow these steps.

1 Start your binding in the middle of one side of the quilt. Leave an 8" to 10" space on the quilt between the beginning and end of the binding. Leave an 8" tail at the beginning and end of the binding strip.

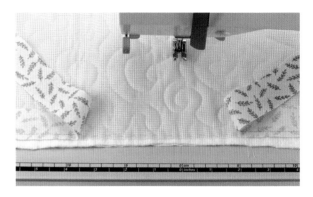

2 On a flat surface, have the binding ends meet in the center of the unstitched space, leaving a scant ¼" space between them. Fold the ends under at that point.

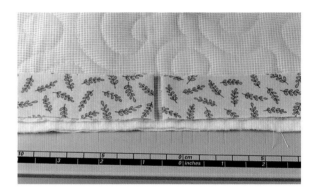

3 Cut off one end at the fold. Then, using the end you have cut off (open it, if it is a double binding) use it to measure a *binding's width* from the fold. Cut off the second end at that point.

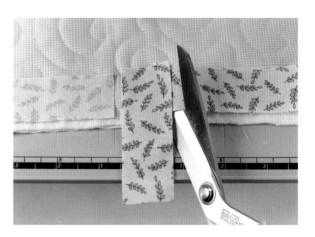

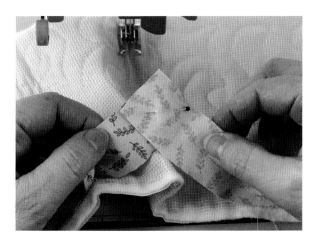

④ Join the ends at right angles with right sides together. Stitch a diagonal seam. Check to make sure the seam has been sewn properly, then trim to ¼". Finger press and reposition the binding on the quilt.

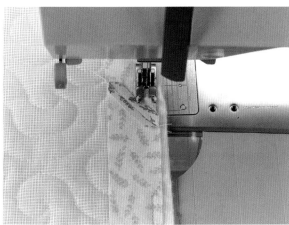

⑤ Finish stitching the binding to the edge of the quilt.

Edge Finishes

Marking

Any curved or shaped quilt edge needs to be marked before binding. I recommend using a blue washout pen. (It allows you to change the markings.) Spritz with water, wait until it dries, and try again.

1 A way to preview a curved or shaped quilt edge is to cut a length of calculator tape the length of the side of your quilt. Mark the scallop, curved or shaped edge on the paper. Cut out and use as a template to mark your quilt edge.

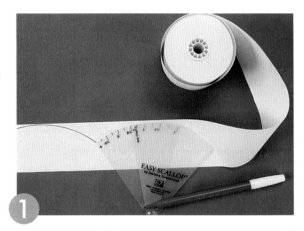

2 You can mark a scalloped, curved or shaped edge with any lid, plate or bowl from your kitchen, or use a compass to achieve the right curve. A helpful *adjustable* tool designed specifically for marking scallops and curves is Easy Scallop.

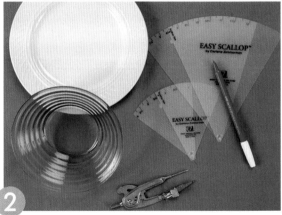

3 The Easy Scallop needs to be assembled before using it the first time. Bend the tabs at the bottom of one half of the tool *up* and insert through the hole on the matching piece. Flatten the tabs. Do the same for the remaining tool.

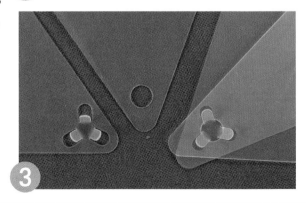

4 The Easy Scallop has a tab that can lock it into place at a particular size. The tools are marked at ¼" intervals and are easily adjustable from 4" to 12".

The scalloped, curved or shaped edge can be marked either **before** or **after** quilting.

5 The scalloped, curved or shaped edge can be marked either *before* or *after* quilting. It can be a last minute decision *after* the quilt has been quilted, or it can be marked before the quilting is done. Perhaps a quilting motif could be added into the curved edge shapes.

6 A scalloped border also can be made to fit the blocks in a quilt. Set the Easy Scallop (or mark intervals) the size of the finished block, centering the scallop over

the block. The corner scallops will end up the width of the border and do not need to be the same size as the rest of the scallops.

Scalloped Edge with Rounded Corners

You can choose which corner treatment, listed in the next section, will fit best with *your* quilt.

A scalloped edge is NOT difficult to mark. Follow this step-by-step procedure and you'll see just how easy it is!

1 Measure the quilt border from edge to edge.

2 The next step is to choose the *number of scallops* you want on the edge. To do this, simply take your finger and "air draw" the scallops along that edge. How many scallops did you draw?

3 Take the length of the quilt edge and divide by the *number of scallops*. That will yield the *size* of the scallops.

EXAMPLE
The quilt edge measures
54½".
I chose 6 scallops.
54½" divided by 6
= 9.0833.

4 Round the answer from Step 3 to the nearest quarter inch (9¼"). Set your Easy Scallop tool to that measurement. If not using Easy Scallop, move on to the next step.

5 Begin marking right at the corner of the quilt. (You can mark right to the edge, as you will be sewing ¼" below the marked line.) Mark the first scallop with Easy Scallop, making sure that you have the same amount of indent at each end of the tool. If not using Easy Scallop, measure off increments of the size chosen in Step 3, and mark the curve with a lid, plate or compass. (The trick is finding the right size.)

6 Mark scallops in the same manner from both corners toward the center, adjusting the middle scallop(s) as needed. The Easy Scallop tool is infinitely adjustable. If you find you have to adjust too much in the center, then go back and check your math — you probably didn't divide accurately. (And, with the blue washout marker, spritz the line with cold water, wait until it dries, and try again.) Mark the *opposite* border in the same way.

Scalloped Edge with
Rounded Corners

7 Usually a quilt is rectangular. If so, you need to refigure the size of the scallops for the remaining two borders. It makes sense if the two remaining borders are longer than the ones just marked, you will need one or more additional scallops along that edge. Follow Steps 1 through 6 again. If the quilt is rectangular, the size of the scallop for the longer sides can be slightly different than the scallop size for the top and bottom of the quilt. As long as the scallop size stays within an inch more or less of the first scallop size, it will look fine. The scallop sizes for the top and bottom of the quilt do NOT need to be the same as for the sides of the quilt, but they do need to be similar.

EXAMPLE

The quilt measures 54½" x 76½".
We've marked the 54½" top
and bottom edge. To mark the side edges,
I will choose 8 scallops (remember, I used 6
scallops at the top and bottom).
76½" divided by 8 = 9.5625.
Set the Easy Scallop tool at 9½" (or mark
intervals at that size). Mark the remaining two
sides of the quilt in the same manner as
Steps 5 and 6 on page 85.
Notice you have automatically
marked a rounded corner.

8 Do NOT cut on the marked line. This line is merely a *placement guide* for the binding. If you cut on the marked line, the quilt would then have a bias edge, which would stretch, fray and distort. Leaving the extra fabric around the scallop ensures the edge is stable for sewing.

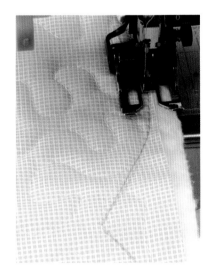

9 When the quilting is completed, baste on that marked line to prevent the layers from shifting when the binding is sewn on. You can hand baste or machine baste (use the longest stitch length) with a walking foot.

Binding a Scalloped Edge

The secret to binding a scalloped edge, without tears, is to use single bias binding cut 1¼" wide. The binding needs to be bias to curve around the scallops, and the single binding is less bulky in the "V's." A single binding is not as durable as a double binding, but consider this — the top layer of a double binding will wear out first and the binding will need to be replaced just as soon as a single binding. And, since we usually give away our quilts, it's NOT OUR PROBLEM!

Refer to pages 74 and 75 for determining your binding amount and preparing the binding.

1 Baste by hand (or with a long stitch and walking foot on the machine) along the marked scalloped edge to keep the layers together.

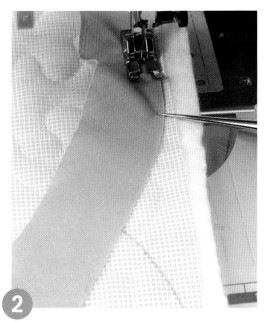

2 Begin at the top of a scallop, leaving at least a 6" to 8" tail. Align the binding strip to the marked edge. Sew a ¼" seam (use your ¼" quilting foot for this task; you've basted, so no need for the walking foot). EASE the binding around the curves. Do not PULL, as this will cause the scallops to cup.

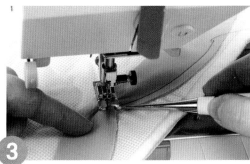

3 Stitch to the bottom of the "V," stop with the needle down, lift the pressure foot, and pivot the quilt and binding around the needle.

A single binding is not as durable as a double binding, but consider this — the top layer of a double binding will wear out first and the binding will need to be replaced just as soon as a single binding. And, since we usually give away our quilts, it's NOT OUR PROBLEM!

4 Push any pleats that form in front of the needle *behind* the needle with a stiletto or seam ripper. Making sure you don't stitch any pleats into the binding, lower the presser foot and stitch out of the "V."

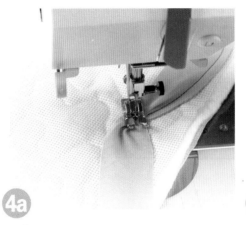

4a

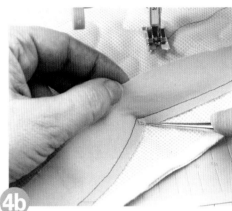

4b

5 Continue around the quilt in this manner. Join the binding ends as shown on page 80.

6 Trim the backing and batting *evenly*, ¼" from the stitching line. Do NOT clip the "V," this will destabilize the scallops and make them floppy.

6

7 Pull the binding to the backside, tuck under ¼", and stitch down by hand with matching thread. If you find that the scallop wants to "cup," you can steam the edges lightly to make them lie flat. (And, next time you'll remember not to PULL the binding around, but EASE instead.) At the "V," the fabric should just fold over upon itself making a small pleat. This pleat will be more or less pronounced, depending upon the sharpness of the "V." You can use a stiletto or the back of your needle to "help" in folding this pleat.

Scalloped Edge with "Ears"

1 Measure the quilt edge. Choose the *number* of scallops. (See Step 2 in Scalloped Edge with Rounded Corners.) Divide the length by the number of scallops to determine the *size* of the scallops. (This is the same procedure you follow for the rounded corners on pages 84 and 85.)

2 Instead of starting with a full scallop at the corners, start with a HALF scallop at the corners. Make sure you have the same amount of indent at both ends of the scallop.

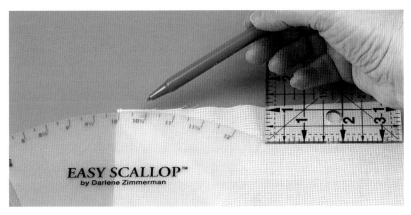

3 Mark from both corners toward the center as before. Adjust the center scallop(s) as needed. Mark opposite edges of the quilt the same way.

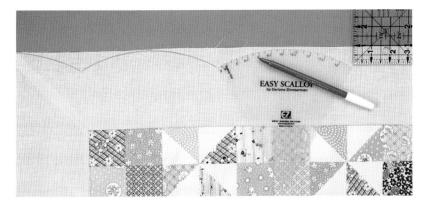

4 Repeat the same procedure for the remaining two sides, remembering to refigure and readjust the scallops if the length is different. (Refer to Step 7 under Scalloped Edge, Rounded Corners on page 86.) Note that the "ears" will automatically happen at the corners.

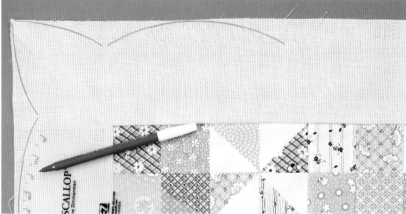

5 When binding "ears," you will need to bind the corners of the quilt with a mitered corner. Refer to page 79 for detailed instructions for mitering binding corners.

◀Buttercup
Fat Quarter Small Quilts

Scalloped Edges with Square Corners

A third option for finishing the corners of a scalloped quilt is to leave them square. To do this, follow the directions for Scalloped Edges with Rounded Corners (pages 84 through 86), but only mark the *inside* of the scallop at the corners, leaving the corners square.

When binding, remember to miter the square corner. Refer to page 79 for detailed instructions for mitering binding corners.

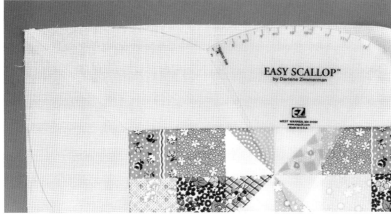

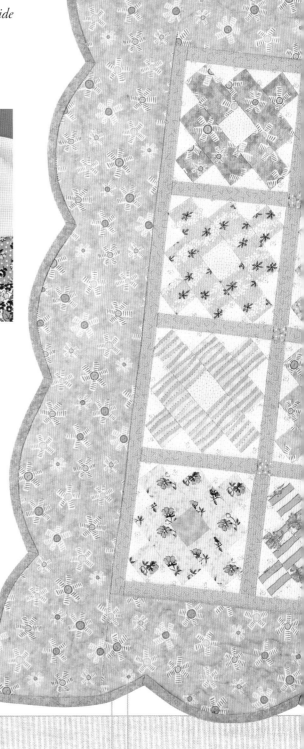

▶Sweet Lavender
Fat Quarter Small Quilts

Notched Edge Finish

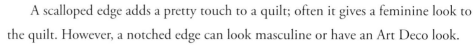

A notched edge is simply a scallop with the top cut off, leaving just the "V" behind.

A scalloped edge adds a pretty touch to a quilt; often it gives a feminine look to the quilt. However, a notched edge can look masculine or have an Art Deco look.

A notched edge is simply a scallop with the top cut off, leaving just the "V" behind.

You can determine where you want the notches to be. They can be aligned with the blocks, as in *Confetti,* or you can make notches the width of your borders, and possibly in the center of each border as well.

1 To mark the notches, make a template from a recipe card. Simply draw in a "V" shape, not more than a 90-degree "V" (as it would be too hard to bind) and about 1" or less deep. See example below.

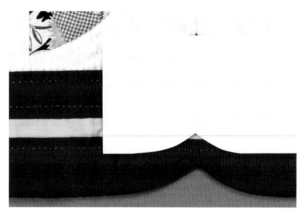

2 Bind with single bias binding, following the steps for binding a scalloped edge on page 87.

Curved Edge Finish – "The Wave"

A softly curved edge with rounded corners is perfect for a small quilt or baby quilt. It also will look quite lush and fancy on a bed quilt. Of all the curved edge finishes, you will find this one the easiest to bind, as there are no "V's" to pivot around.

To mark a curvy (wavy) edge you must choose an UNEVEN number of scallops and use a rather FLAT curve.

1 Measure the quilt from edge to edge.

2 Decide on the number of scallops (curves). Count both the inner and outer curves and remember to choose an UNEVEN number.

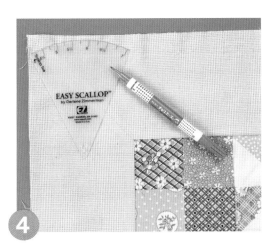

3 Divide the length of the quilt by the number of scallops (curves). Round to the nearest ¼". Set the Easy Scallop tool to that measurement (or, if not using the tool, move on to the next step).

4 Begin marking a full scallop at the edge of the quilt, keeping the same amount of indent on both sides of the tool.

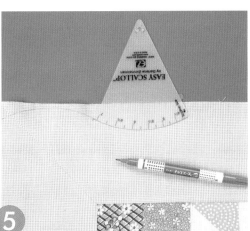

5 Reverse the tool and mark an upside down curve. Check to make sure the indent is the same.

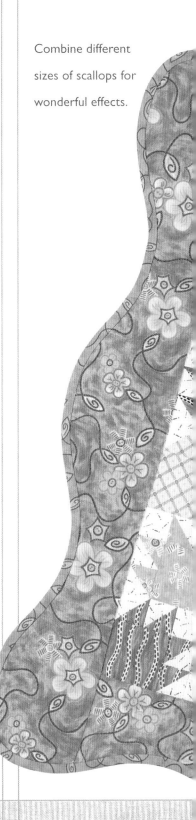

Combine different sizes of scallops for wonderful effects.

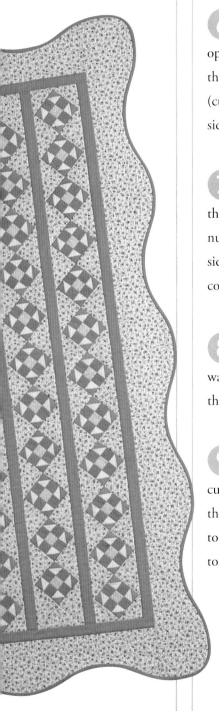

6 Repeat Steps 4 and 5 at the opposite corner, working towards the center. Adjust the middle scallop (curve) as needed. Mark the opposite side the same way.

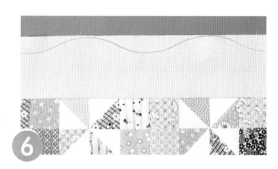

7 Measure, divide the length by the number of scallops (an UNEVEN number) and mark the remaining two sides. You will have a softly rounded corner automatically marked.

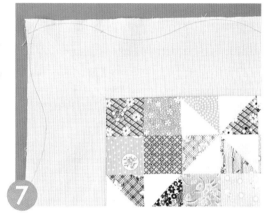

8 Baste by hand (or by using the walking foot on the machine) along the marked line.

9 Bind with single bias binding cut 1¼". EASE the binding around the inside and outside curves. Refer to binding a curved edge on pages 87 to 88.

TIP: You can mix sizes of scallops or curves to change the look of the quilt. Alternate large and small scallops to keep the curves from becoming too extreme. See *A Tisket, A Tasket* at right. I used a large scallop on the outside curves, marking a large scallop at each corner and centering the middle one. I chose a small scallop to fit the space between the large scallops and marked small scallops between the large ones in reverse curves.

Another way to mark a curved edge or "wave," without using any math, is to start by centering a scallop of any size in the middle of a border. Experiment with marking reversed and regular scallops of various sizes, out from the center. Combine different sizes of scallops for wonderful effects. If you get to a corner and the scallop is reversed, making the corner awkward, simply reverse the direction of the center scallop and repeat the procedure. It would be wise to experiment on calculator paper or by "air drawing."

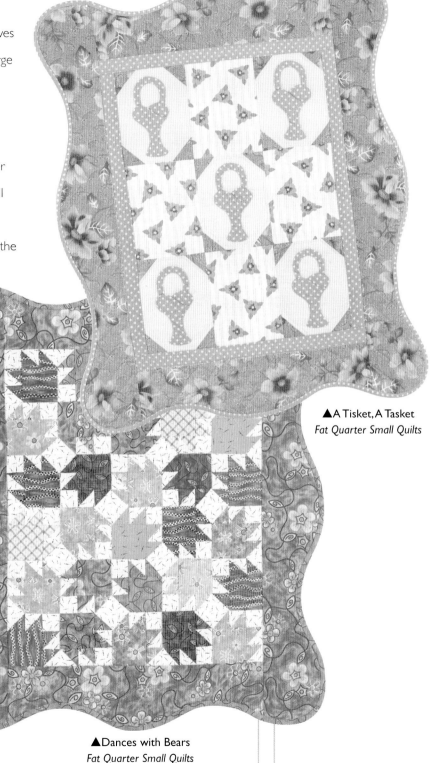

▲A Tisket, A Tasket
Fat Quarter Small Quilts

▲Dances with Bears
Fat Quarter Small Quilts

Free-Form Edges

For an art quilt, or a quilt with a contemporary look, you can design a wonderful free-form curvy border. Simply draw it free hand (remembering not to use more than a 90-degree angle in any "V's"). Or, you can use a tool called Flex Design Rule. It is a flexible ruler that you can bend (and it will stay) in any curvy shape, allowing you to design and mark a curvy border, and repeat it, if you choose to do so, on the remainder of the borders.

Bind a free-form border in the same way as any curved or scalloped border — with single bias binding.

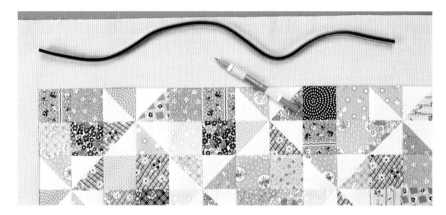

Pre-Shaped Curved Edges

A good example of this type of quilt is the Double Wedding Ring at left. There also are other variations of this pattern that have curved edges. In this case, the curve is already part of the quilt. Hand basting along the curved edge before binding, and careful handling while stitching the binding, will allow you to bind the edge following the steps outlined for binding a scalloped edge (pages 87 to 88). Use a single bias binding for the best results.

Inside Scalloped or Shaped Edge Border

In this instance, a scalloped or shaped edge is appliquéd to another border; and the last border will have a straight edge finish. An inside scalloped or shaped edge border can look very interesting, but involves appliquéing it to the outer border. It forms a lovely frame around a quilt, while allowing you to bind a straight edge.

To begin, sew the first border (or the one to be scalloped or shaped) to the quilt. Miter the corners, if desired. (See page 61 for detailed instructions for mitering border corners.)

▲Sunbonnet Sue
Granny Quilts

Freezer Paper Method

After the first scalloped or shaped border is sewn onto the quilt, but BEFORE the next border is added, follow these steps:

1 Cut one freezer paper strip 3" to 5" wide and the length of the top and bottom borders. Cut another freezer paper strip 3" to 5" wide the length of the side border of the quilt.

TIP: If your freezer paper isn't the correct length, simply overlap the strips about ½" and apply a warm iron to the joint. In this manner you can make a freezer paper strip any length.

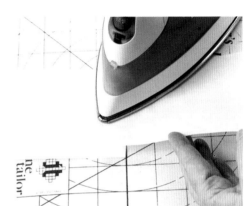

2 Trim the freezer paper strips to exactly the length of your borders. Mark a scalloped or curved edge on the freezer paper strips as if they were the borders. (See page 82 for detailed instructions for marking curved or scalloped edges.) Cut on the marked lines.

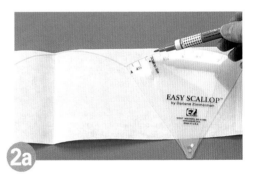

TIP: The freezer paper can be reused several times, so only two freezer paper borders need to be prepared.

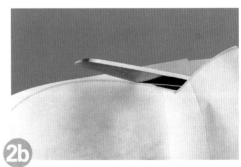

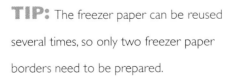

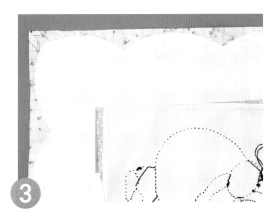

3 Iron the freezer paper borders to the wrong side of the borders to be scalloped on the quilt, with the scalloped or curved shape along the outer edge, but allowing for at least a ¼" seam beyond the freezer paper for a turn-under allowance.

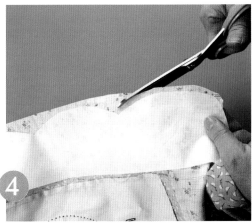

4 Cut out the curved or scalloped edge ¼" beyond the freezer paper. Clip any inside curves.

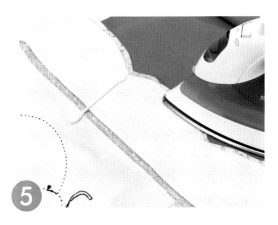

5 Wet the edge of the border fabric with a cotton swab dipped in 1:1 starch and water mixture. Fold and press the raw edge over the edge of the freezer paper. Repeat for all the borders.

TIP: It doesn't matter if the outer border is wider than needed, it can be trimmed later.

6 Cut the outer border fabric strips. To figure what width to cut these border strips, take the width you want to show plus 2" extra to tuck under the scalloped or shaped inside border.

7 Cut the border length to allow for mitered corners (see page 61 for detailed instructions for mitering border corners). Lay the outer borders under the shaped or scalloped border. Make sure they are tucked under the scalloped or shaped borders. Baste in place. Finish the corners of the last border by mitering or making butted corners.

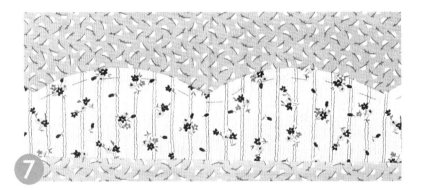

8 Appliqué the scalloped or shaped border to the outer border by hand or machine. After the appliqué is complete, trim away any excess outer border fabric if it shadows through under the scalloped or shaped border.

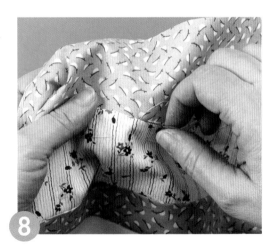

9 Quilt as desired. Bind the straight edge according to the directions on page 76.

Needle-turn Method

1 The inside border is marked with a scalloped or curved edge. The border edge can be marked as in the steps for marking a scalloped or curved edge outlined on pages 82 and 83. This must be done after the border is sewn to the quilt, but BEFORE the outer border is added. After the scalloped edge is marked, it is cut ¼" **above** the marked line.

2 To determine the width to cut the outer scalloped or shaped borders, take the width you want to show plus 2" for overlapping under the scalloped or shaped border. It doesn't matter if the border is wider than needed, it can be trimmed later.

3 Cut the outer borders longer than needed to allow for mitering corners.

4 The outer (last) border is basted *under* the shaped edge, overlapping an inch or more, so it is completely under the scalloped or shaped edge.

The corners of the outer (last) border can be finished off with mitered or butted corners.

5 The scalloped border is needle-turned under **on** the marked line and appliquéd to the outer border. The appliqué is stitched by hand, then the excess fabric of the outer border underneath is trimmed off.

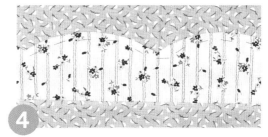

6 Quilt as desired. Bind the outer (last) border (straight edge) as described on page 76.

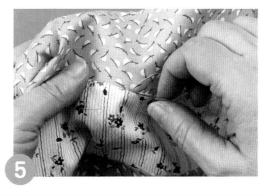

Adding a Flange to a Binding

NOTE: If sewing a
flange to a straight-
edge quilt, the flange
can be cut from
straight-of-grain
fabric. If sewing the
flange to a curved or
scalloped edge, you
will need to cut bias
strips.

Adding a flange to your quilt can bring out one of the colors of your quilt and greatly increase the visual appeal of your binding. A flange is not difficult to add, just follow these steps:

Appliqué design and hand-dyed fabrics by Dianne Johnston.
Project made by author.

1 Hand baste a scant ¼" from the edge of the quilt to keep the layers from shifting. Cut the fabric for a flange ¾" wide (this is correct and not a typo!) and the length of each side of the quilt (after it's been quilted). Fold the flange in half *lengthwise* and press with *wrong* sides together.

2 Sew the prepared flange to the top and bottom of the quilt with a scant ¼" seam. Sew a flange to all sides of the quilt in the same manner, overlapping at the corners.

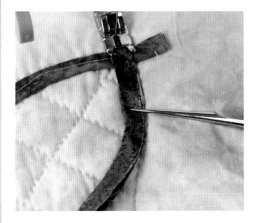

3 Sew the prepared binding to the quilt with a ¼" seam, mitering the corners. (See page 76 for directions for stitching on a binding and page 79 for mitering corners.) Stitch as **accurately** as possible, as this will determine the width of the flange when finished.

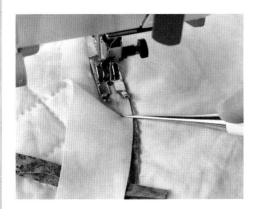

4 Trim excess batting and backing. Turn the binding to the backside and stitch down by hand.

5 If you'd like a different width of flange or width of finished binding, this is the formula you need: Seam width + width of flange that shows = A. A x 2 = width to cut flange.

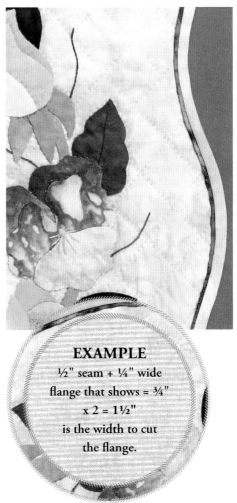

EXAMPLE
½" seam + ¼" wide
flange that shows = ¾"
x 2 = 1½"
is the width to cut
the flange.

Prairie Points

A prairie point edging can be the perfect finish for some quilts. It can be a nice way to finish off a scrap quilt by incorporating the fabrics from the quilt itself in the edging. Or, all of the prairie points can be the same color and be used to repeat a design element from within the quilt.

▲Sweet Memories
Granny Quilts

▲Parasol Ladies
Granny Quilt Décor

WARNING!

Prairie points

must be added

to the quilt

BEFORE quilting!

Prairie points

are a surprisingly

easy edge finish,

but the proper

sequence must

be followed, or

you will have

a big problem

when you get

to the last step!

(Don't ask me

how I know

this…!)

Preparing the Prairie Points

1 Cut squares from a variety of prints or the color of your choice. The square can be any size, generally from 2" to 5". Experiment with different size squares to find a size you like.

2 Fold a square once on the diagonal. Press. Fold again on the diagonal. Press. Repeat with each of the squares.

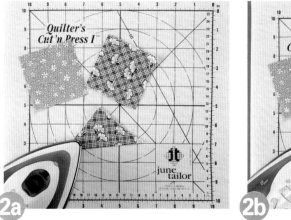 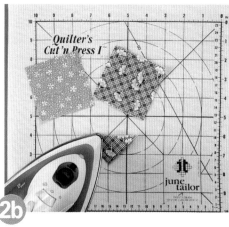

3 Tuck the folded end of one prairie point inside another, with at least ¼" overlap at the base. (It can be more than ¼".) Baste together with a scant ¼" seam (by machine with the longest stitch) a continuous border of prairie points the length of your quilt edge. (At this point the quilt should NOT be quilted!) The prairie points should come exactly to the corners of the quilt top.

4 Sew the prairie points to the quilt top. Use a ¼" seam, a regular stitch length and the prairie points just touching at the corners. At this point the prairie points are all facing in towards the center of the quilt.

TIP: To make the prairie points fit the quilt edge exactly, remove a few basting stitches, adjust the prairie points closer or further apart, then re-baste. Do this as needed in several places.

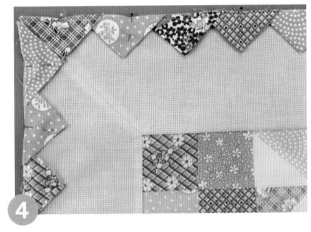

5 Layer, baste and quilt, staying about 1" from the edge of the quilt. (Don't stitch over the prairie points.)

6 Lay the quilt on a flat surface and trim the backing and batting even with the raw edge of the quilt top (or, if you prefer more turn-under, cut ¼" longer).

7 Trim the batting only, about ¼" shorter than the quilt top.

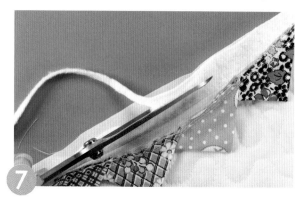

8 Turn the prairie points to the outside of the quilt. The batting should tuck under the seam on the backside.

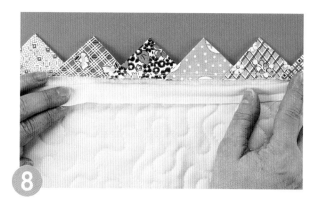

9 Turn the backing fabric under approximately ¼", so that it covers the line of stitching. Trim excess bulk at the corners. Stitch down by hand with matching thread.

10 Finish any quilting along the prairie point edge, if needed.

Continuous Prairie Points

This may be a method you never use, but make yourself a sample — you will impress your quilting friends.

When making prairie points all the same color or alternating two colors, you can use the following method to make them from a strip of fabric.

1 To make a *sample*, cut an 8" x 21" strip of fabric. Mark a line exactly down the center of the 21" length of fabric strip.

2 On one half side of the strip mark off 4" intervals.

3 On the other half of the strip, measure 2" in and mark off in 4" intervals.

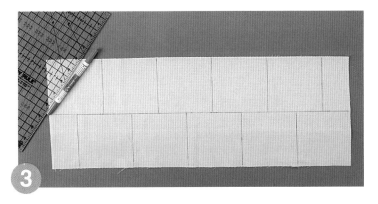

4 Cut off and discard the 2" x 4" piece on each side. Cut up to the center on the remainder of the marked lines.

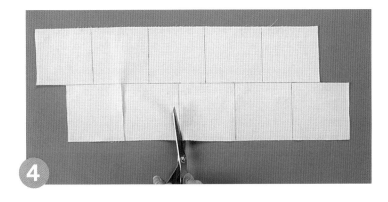

TIP: If you have the folded edge in the wrong place on your prairie points, you won't be able to tuck one inside the other. This will happen if you fold the wrong direction on your first fold. Go back and refold correctly.

5 Fold the squares on the diagonal, first to the left, then to the right. Press.

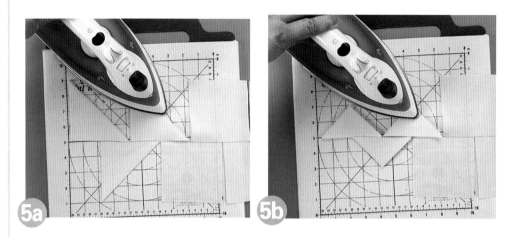

6 Repeat for each of the squares, then tuck one inside the other, making a continuous line of prairie points. Baste a scant ¼" along the base of the prairie points.

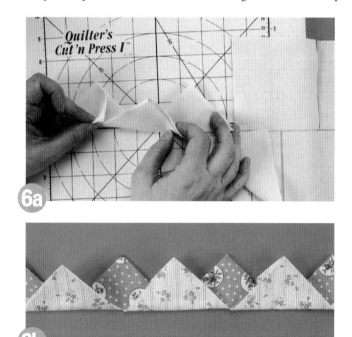

You can achieve another look with the prairie points by NOT tucking them at all. Then alternate prairie points will either be in front of or behind the others.

Two-Color Prairie Points

Two-color prairie points also are possible using this method.

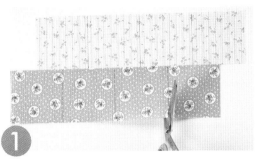

1 Cut two different strips of fabric 4¼" wide, then sew together along the long edge. Press.

2 Mark, cut and fold the two halves of the strip following the steps as outlined in Steps 1 through 6 on pages 109 and 110.

Formula for Making a Continuous Prairie Point Edging

With this method, it is very important the prairie point strip is exactly the length of your quilt top. It is NOT adjustable, as in the individual prairie point method. The prairie points made with this method are permanently connected. To ensure your prairie points fit your quilt, determine the length and the width of the strip and then cut accordingly. The formula is as follows:

EXAMPLE
Your quilt measures 39½" square.
The strip measurement divides nearly evenly by 3. (3 x 2 = 6".)
This is the *width* of the strip to cut.
Cut your strips 6" x 39½".
Mark off 3" intervals (and mark the second side starting 1½" in) but mark a few of them slightly wider to accommodate the extra ½".

1 Measure the length of the quilt top; this is the *length* you will need to cut your strip. (You may need to piece the strip to get the proper length.)

2 Find a number between two and five that will divide evenly (or as close as you can get it) into the *length* of your strip.

3 Take that number **x 2** to equal the *width* of the strip.

4 Measure, mark, cut and fold as directed on pages 109 and 110, and finish according to the directions for a prairie point edge.

Knife-Edge Finish

The best option for the irregular edge on a Grandmother's Flower Garden quilt is a knife-edge finish.

Some quilts, such as Grandmother's Flower Garden, naturally have an uneven edge finish. One then has the option of trimming the edge straight, appliquéing it onto a border as in Inside Scalloped or Shaped Edges, (pages 97-101) or keeping the edge intact with a knife-edge finish. Trying to bind a hexagon edge would be a daunting task — all those inside and outside miters! Because of the difficult edge finish on Grandmother's Flower Garden quilts, we find many of them unfinished. The best option for the irregular edge on a Grandmother's Flower Garden quilt is a knife-edge finish. It is not hard to do, and it's an effective way to finish an irregular edge and keep it intact.

To make a knife-edge finish on *any* irregular edge, follow these steps:

1 Leave the irregular edge until last. Layer, baste and quilt as desired, leaving the last row of hexagons around the edge unquilted.

2 Lay the quilt on a flat surface and trim the batting and backing even with the edge of the quilt top.

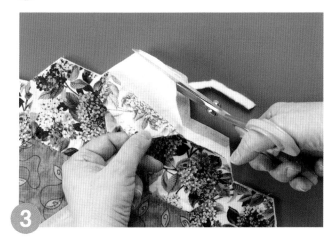

3 Trim the batting ¼" *less* than the quilt top.

<hr />

Knife-Edge Finish

4 Fold the backing and quilt top edges in ¼". The folded edges should just meet. Whipstitch the edges by hand with matching thread.

5 Finish any quilting along the edge.

Ice Cream Cone Border

Ice cream cone borders are a unique edge finish found on '30s era quilts, most frequently seen on Dresden Plate quilts. Usually an ice cream cone border has a print alternated with a white or background upside down "cone."

The "ice cream cones" can be any length or width on the border of a quilt, and the angle can change. However, to make the border lie flat and straight (not curved) the ice cream cone and background cone pieces need to have the same *angle*. The angle can be whatever you choose. They can differ in width, but the *angles* of the two different cone pieces need to be the same. You can use an acrylic tool to help you cut a 60-degree angle (or a different angle) for both pieces, or you can use the templates supplied on page 117.

1 "Ice cream cones" can have flat or rounded edges, with the rounded edges being the most popular. Cut a print "ice cream cone" with the round template, and use background fabric with the flat top template.

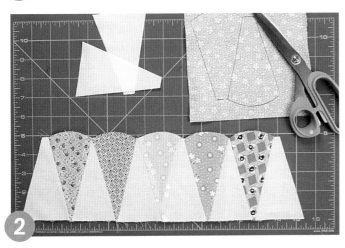

2 Sew together with wide edges opposite one another.

3 There is no easy way to work out the mathematics of the ice cream cone border. You simply have to sew as many "ice cream cones" as needed for the correct border length. It is somewhat adjustable by taking in or letting out a few seams across the border. Note the corners do not make a right angle, but four cones together will fill out a corner.

4 Another way to adjust the ice cream cone border to fit your quilt is to add a wider inside border — either from the background color or a contrasting color. Cut the inside border a bit wider than needed, so you can trim evenly to make the quilt fit the border. See page 67 for more tips on how to do that.

5 Once the border has been sewn to all sides of the quilt, you can layer, baste and quilt as desired. The gentle curve of the print "ice cream cones" forms a shallow scallop border. Hand baste a scant ¼" along the outside edge to stabilize the bias edge and to keep the layers from shifting. Bind using a single bias binding. See page 87 for detailed instructions for binding a scalloped border, and pages 71 through 75 for cutting and preparing a single bias binding.

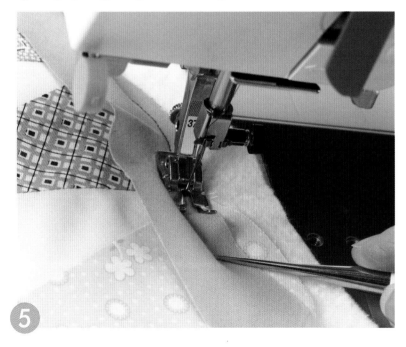

Ice Cream Cone
Border

Quilt Labels

A label can be as

simple as writing

your name

somewhere

on the quilt in

permanent fabric

ink, or it can be

as elaborate as

you want it to

be.

Now that you have learned many new techniques for bordering and finishing the edge of your quilt, you will want to get ALL of your projects finished, right? When you do finish a project, be sure to **label** it for future generations.

A label can be as simple as writing your name somewhere on the quilt in permanent fabric ink, or it can be as elaborate as you want it to be. Put yourself in your great-granddaughter's shoes for a moment. She just "discovered" your quilt for the first time, she's curious as to who made it, and that information should all be on the label. Is it enough just to have your name on the quilt? No, she'll want to know WHEN you made the quilt, WHO it was made for, WHY this person was given a quilt, WHERE you lived at the time you made it, and so on. Answer all those questions on a label and generations yet to be born will thank you!

Labels can be printed with permanent ink on a printer, handwritten with permanent fabric pens, embroidered by hand or machine, or even written on paper and stored with the quilt. Labels attached to a quilt however, are more likely to stay with the quilt, as a document could be lost. Pre-made quilt labels also are available to purchase by the yard in quilt shops, or you can make your own. The label is usually attached to the back of the quilt with hand applique after the quilt is finished, or, if you remember, attach it to the *backing* before layering and quilting. The quilting will ensure it stays in place.

Hanging Sleeve

A hanging sleeve is used for hanging your quilt. It is added after a quilt is finished. I prefer to make the hanging sleeve from leftover backing fabric; but in reality, the hanging sleeve won't show, so it doesn't matter what fabric you use.

For a small wall hanging, the sleeve only needs to be wide enough to accommodate a slender dowel; for a large, heavy quilt, the dowel or flat wood piece (similar to a yardstick) needs to be stronger, and the sleeve larger to accommodate it.

Usually, double the width of the dowel or wood piece is a generous sleeve width. Add ½" if you are going to turn under the long edges on both sides. The length of the sleeve should be slightly less than the width of the quilt (you don't want it to show) and the dowel or wood piece needs to extend beyond the sleeve in order to rest on nails or connect to a quilt holder.

If desired, press the long and short ends under ¼ inch, and stitch down with matching thread. The sleeve is basted by hand to the back layers of the quilt, not through to the front of the quilt. Hand basting will allow you to easily remove the sleeve at a later date.

A larger quilt (lap or larger) should have another sleeve and dowel at the bottom of the quilt to allow it to hang flat against the wall. If the quilt is not directional, and can be turned any direction, you could add a sleeve on all four sides and rotate the quilt occasionally.

> I prefer to make the hanging sleeve from leftover backing fabric; but in reality, the hanging sleeve won't show, so it doesn't matter what fabric you use.

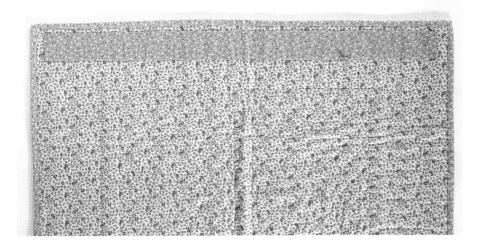

Finishing a Pillow

Pillow Backing

Double-layer pillow backs are easy to make and have more body than a single-layer pillow back. To figure what size to cut the pillow backs, add 5" to the unfinished size of the pillow top for overlap, and cut two pillow backs to that size.

1 Fold the pillow backs in half so each measures 16½" x 10¾". Press.

2 Overlap the folded edges of the pillow back pieces so they make a pillow back measuring 16½". Machine baste (using a long stitch) a scant ¼" around the edge of the pillow to hold the back pieces together.

3 Sew the pillow top and pillow backs with right sides together and a generous ¼" seam. Round the corners slightly for a nice finish on the front side. Insert the pillow form through the folded opening on the backside.

Ruffles

Most pillows look attractive with a ruffle. To figure the cut width size of your ruffle strips, first decide what size finished ruffle you need. Add ¼" (for seam allowance) and multiply by 2. This gives you the finished width to cut.

To determine the length of the ruffle, figure the circumference of the pillow (the measurement of all four sides). Take that number and multiply by 2.5. This will tell you how many inches of ruffle fabric to cut. Divide that number by 40", round to the nearest whole number, and you will have the number of strips you need to cut and piece together.

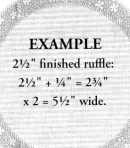

1 Piece the ruffle strips right sides together with diagonal seams pressed open. Join the ends into a continuous circle. Fold the ruffle in half lengthwise with wrong sides together and press.

2 Fold the ruffle length in half so you have a fold at each end. Place a safety pin at the raw edge of each end. Fold it in half again; place safety pins at the folds (quarter points). Unfold.

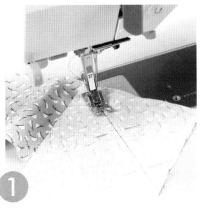

3 Gather the ruffle by stitching two rows of basting (longest stitch on your machine) close together, a scant ¼" from the edge. Pull the bobbin thread from both ends to gather. The safety pin markers on the ruffle should match up with the corners of your pillow. Gather and pin in place.

4 Before sewing the ruffle to your pillow top, decide whether or not you want to add quilting to your pillow top. If so, the time to quilt is BEFORE you add the ruffle.

5 Pin the ruffle to the pillow top with the ruffle facing in.

6 Sew the ruffle to the pillow top with a basting stitch (the longest stitch on your sewing machine), and a ¼" seam, making certain there is enough fullness in the ruffle at the corners. You may find it easier to slightly round the corners with the ruffle.

7 Layer the pillow top, right sides together, with the pillow back (see page 120 for detailed instructions on making a double-fold pillow back). The ruffle should now be sandwiched in between the top and back. Stitch a generous ¼" seam at a regular stitch length, and round the corners, if you desire. Trim the corners after stitching.

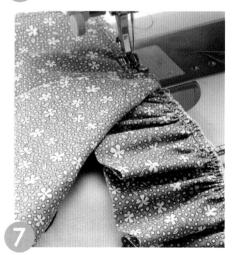

8 Turn the pillow right-side out through the opening in the back and fluff up the ruffle. Insert the pillow form.

Faux Double Ruffle

A double ruffle is an extra-special, extra-full ruffle treatment for a pillow, but it's a real pain to insert all the thickness in the seam allowance. Instead of making two ruffles, simply *piece the ruffle fabrics* and fold in half to make a double ruffle. For example: If you want a ruffle that finishes to 3" with 1" of the second color showing around the edge, cut one strip at 2½" and the second color strip at 4½". If you change the finished size of your ruffle, cut one ruffle strip approximately 2" wider than the first ruffle strip. Together they should measure 2 times the finished width, plus 1" for the seam allowances. Sew and finish, as for the single ruffle.

Appliquéd pillow made by Lyn Voigt.

Pillow with a Flange (Flat Ruffle)

A flange is an easy way to add an interesting edge to your pillow. Simply add a border around the edge of the pillow top. It can be contrasting like the usual border, or the same as the background, so it looks like a continuation of the block. Quilt the pillow top, if desired.

Make a backing as large as the top, sew right sides together and turn. Lay the pillow flat. Pin the front and back together along the border. Stitch around the pillow in the ditch, between the pillow and the border, creating a flange, or an ungathered ruffle. Refer to page 120 for detailed instructions for making a double-fold pillow backing.

Pillow with Binding

The easiest way to finish a pillow with a professional edge treatment is to simply bind it. The binding can look like cording, without all the work! It's a good idea to have at least a small border around the pillow top, as you will be sewing a ⅜" seam for the binding.

1 Piece, layer and quilt (if desired) the pillow top. Hand baste ¼" from the edge of the pillow top to keep the layers from shifting.

2 Baste the pillow top and pillow back, with wrong sides together, using the longest stitch on your sewing machine.

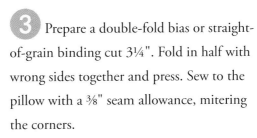

3 Prepare a double-fold bias or straight-of-grain binding cut 3¼". Fold in half with wrong sides together and press. Sew to the pillow with a ⅜" seam allowance, mitering the corners.

4 Trim excess batting and backing. Turn to the backside and stitch down by hand with matching thread.

Resources

The tools and supplies shown in this book are from the following manufacturers and can be found at your local quilt shop, fabric or craft store, on the Web or by mail order.

Clotilde, LLC
P.O. Box 7500
Big Sandy, TX 75755-7500
(800) 772-2891
www.clotilde.com

Connecting Threads
P.O. Box 870760
Vancouver, WA 98687-7760
(800) 574-6454
www.ConnectingThreads.com

EZ Quilting by Wrights
85 South Street
P.O. Box 398
West Warren, MA 01092
(800) 660-0415
www.ezquilt.com
Flip-n-Set
Easy Scallop
Easy Rule
Flex Design Rule
Binding Clips

Home Sew
P.O. Box 4099
Bethlehem, PA 18018-0099
(800) 344-4739
www.homesew.com

June Tailor, Inc.
P.O. Box 208
Hwy. 175
Richfield, WI 53076
(800) 844-5400
Cut & Press I

Keepsake Quilting
Route 25
P.O. Box 1618
Center Harbor, NH 03226-1618
(800) 438-5464
www.keepsakequilting.com

Nancy's Notions
333 Beichl Ave
P.O. Box 683
Beaver Dam, WI 53916-0683
(800) 833-0690
www.nancysnotions.com

Books

KP Books
An Imprint of F+W Publications
700 East State Street
Iola, WI 54990-001
(715) 445-2214
(888) 457-2873
www.krause.com

Projects for any Décor

by Darlene Zimmerman

Granny Quilts

Vintage Quilts of the '30s Made New for Today
This full-color pattern book offers 19 projects for creating quilts that replicate the look of the popular quilts of the 1930s. Features a variety of appliquéd and pieced quilts.

Softcover • 8¼ x 10⅞ • 128 pages
25 full-size templates
70 color photos & 165 illus.
Item# GRANQ • $21.95

Granny Quilt Décor

Vintage Quilts of the '30s inspire projects for today's home
Features quilting ideas for all skill levels, including bed-size quilts, wall hangings, pillows, kitchen novelties and more. Includes over 30 fantastic projects and basic quilting instructions, as well as a fascinating historical look at these '30s era quilts.

Softcover • 8¼ x 10⅞ • 128 pages
125 color photos, 150 illus.
Item# GQDCR • $21.99

Quick Quilted Miniatures

Quilters of all skill levels will learn how to easily create miniature quilts without an exorbitant amount of time. Offers step-by-step instructions for creating quick miniatures and 38 designs for all seasons.

Softcover • 8¼ x 10⅞ • 128 pages
40 color photos, 140 illus.
Item# QQM • $21.95

Fat Quarter Small Quilts

25 Projects You Can Make in a Day
Using "fat quarters," quilters will complete 25 projects including wall hangings, tablemats, doll quilts, gifts and more in a wide variety of themes. Most projects can be completed in less than a day!

Softcover • 8¼ x 10⅞ • 128 pages
75+ color photos, 100 illus.
Item# FQSM • $21.99

Barbara Randle's More Crazy Quilting with Attitude

by Barbara Randle

Three techniques enable quilters and sewers to create 14 trendy crazy-quilting projects, including a throw, diaper bag, a variety of handbags and a gallery of customized clothing. Ideal for all skill-levels with full-size patterns included.

Softcover • 8¼ x 10⅞
128 pages
200+ color photos,
60+ illus.
**Item# CQWA2
$23.99**

New Country Quilting

25 Pieced and Appliqued Projects
by Denise Clason

Using softer, lighter colors, quilters can create more than 20 projects in coordinating designs for any room in the home. Simple step-by-step instructions and more than 100 color photos transform a room from drab to fresh in no time.

Softcover • 8¼ x 10⅞
128 pages
100 color photos, 75 illus.
**Item# NCQH
$21.99**

Incorporate Today's Hottest Trends and Techniques into Hundreds of Projects

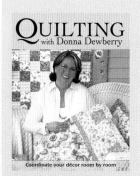

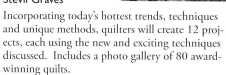